国际篮联裁判员手册
个人执裁技术

中国篮球协会 审定

北京体育大学出版社

策划编辑：曾 莉
责任编辑：曾 莉 吴海燕
责任校对：张志富
版式设计：高文函

图书在版编目（CIP）数据

国际篮联裁判员手册. 个人执裁技术 / 中国篮球协会审定. -- 北京：北京体育大学出版社，2021.9（2024.7重印）
ISBN 978-7-5644-3496-0

Ⅰ.①国… Ⅱ.①中… Ⅲ.①篮球运动—裁判法—手册 Ⅳ.① G841.4-62

中国版本图书馆 CIP 数据核字（2021）第 189992 号

国际篮联裁判员手册：个人执裁技术 中国篮球协会 审定

出版发行：	北京体育大学出版社
地 址：	北京市海淀区农大南路1号院2号楼2层办公B-212
邮 编：	100084
网 址：	http://cbs.bsu.edu.cn
发 行 部：	010-62989320
邮 购 部：	北京体育大学出版社读者服务部 010-62989432
印 刷：	河北盛世彩捷印刷有限公司
开 本：	880mm×1230mm 1/32
成品尺寸：	145mm×210mm
印 张：	4
字 数：	111千字
版 次：	2021年11月第1版
印 次：	2024年7月第4次印刷
定 价：	29.00元

（本书如有印刷质量问题，请与出版社联系调换）

版权所有·侵权必究

出版说明

- 《国际篮联裁判员手册：个人执裁技术》由中国篮球协会依照国际篮球联合会（简称"国际篮联"）发布的 FIBA Referees Manual 翻译和修订。今后所有正式国际篮球比赛和国内篮球比赛，以及各类篮球裁判员晋级考试，均按最新《篮球规则》及《国际篮联裁判员手册》执行。

- 《国际篮联裁判员手册：个人执裁技术》的翻译和编订力求忠实于原文。如在理解和执行过程中出现争议，以国际篮联官方语言英文版为准。翻译和审校工作可能存在疏漏之处，欢迎广大读者提出意见和建议，以便我们及时修订和完善。

- 整本《国际篮联裁判员手册：个人执裁技术》中所有提到的教练员、运动员、技术官员等都是男性，同样也适用于女性。必须强调，这样写只是为了实用的缘故。

FOREWORD

Basketball, as a game, is progressing in skill and speed every day. It is a natural environmental development process that takes place unconditionally and it is called evolution. The game and more so refereeing has completely changed from 10 years ago. Presently, top level refereeing is improving at least at the same speed as the game itself and higher standards of performance are expected every year. The pace of change has necessitated the adoption of a motto: "What was considered exceptionally good yesterday, is considered standard quality today and below average quality tomorrow".

This manual complements other FIBA technical manuals for officiating. The Individual Officiating Techniques (IOT) Manual provides the foundation of successful basketball refereeing, namely to referee one play situation at a time.

The content in this IOT Manual content should be considered as a basic standard of mechanical and technical procedures that are executed individually on the court and every referee at FIBA level should have the detailed know-how.

To enhance the IOT skills, referees are expected to train and practice these techniques in their own time, both on and off the court. This should be done in pursuit of mastering your skills - remembering of course that thousands of repetitions are needed to develop muscle memory. This makes the difference between a good referee and a top elite level referee and generates a standard operational level regardless of the games or environment.

In addition FIBA Referee Operations produce a variety of supporting material, namely "Improve Your" series (for example 'Improve Your Lead Positioning'). These guides provide more insight and details on how to work with the content mentioned in this manual.

前 言

篮球作为一项运动，在技术和速度上每天都在进步，它是一种自然发展过程，无条件发生，被称为演变。比赛本身以及执裁方式与10年前完全不同。目前，顶级的执裁方式的进展速度快于篮球比赛本身，并且每年都有更高的裁判规范标准。目前的发展速度使我们树立了一个座右铭："过去被视为极好的标准，在当前是普通标准，到了将来会低于平均标准。"

这本手册是针对其他国际篮联执裁相关的技术手册的补充。个人执裁技术（IOT）为成功的篮球执裁奠定了基础，也因"一个时刻执裁一个比赛情况"而得名。

该个人执裁技术手册内容应当被视为是每一名具备国际篮联水准的裁判员在场上场下都应通晓并执行的关于裁判法和技术标准的基本标准。

为了提高个人执裁技术能力，我们期望所有裁判员在场上场下都利用他们的时间去训练并实践这些技术。需要持之以恒才能做到极致，通过成千上万次的重复才能生成的肌肉记忆。这也是区分优秀裁判员和顶尖裁判员的标准，同时也建立了标准化的运行体系，无论比赛环境是好是坏。

此外，国际篮联裁判运管部提供各种配套支持材料，例如"提高你的……"系列（例如"提高你的前导占位"）。这些指导文件都在本手册的基础上提供给裁判员更多执裁工作中的理念和细节。

TABLE OF CONTENTS

CHAPTER 1

1.	**GENERAL**	2
1.1	BASKETBALL OFFICIATING	2
1.2	IMAGE OF AN ELITE BASKETBALL REFEREE	2

CHAPTER 2

2.	**INDIVIDUAL OFFICIATING TECHNIQUES (IOT)**	8
2.1	INTRODUCTION	8
2.2	DISTANCE & STATIONARY	10
2.3	REFEREEING THE DEFENCE	12
2.4	STAY WITH THE PLAY	14
2.5	POSITIONING, OPEN ANGLE (45°) AND ADJUSTMENTS	16
2.6	PRE-GAME CONFERENCE AND USE OF FIBA IREF PG APP	18
2.7	MAKING A CALL, DECISION MAKING AND COMMUNICATION	22
2.8	SIGNALS & REPORTING	26
2.9	JUMP BALL / ACTIVE REFEREE (TOSSING THE BALL)	32
2.10	JUMP BALL / NON-ACTIVE REFEREE(S)	34
2.11	COVERING A SHOT (PROTECT THE SHOOTER)	34
2.12	THROW-IN ADMINISTRATION (GENERAL & FRONTCOURT ENDLINE)	36
2.13	FAKE A FOUL	38
2.14	CONTROL OF THE GAME AND SHOT CLOCK	44

CHAPTER 3

3.	**SIGNALS & TERMINOLOGY**	52
3.1	OFFICIAL REFEREES' SIGNALS	52
3.2	BASIC BASKETBALL OFFICIATING TERMINOLOGY	70

目录

第 1 章

1. 通则   3
1.1 篮球比赛执裁   3
1.2 精英篮球裁判员的形象   3

第 2 章

2. 个人执裁技术（IOT）   9
2.1 引言   9
2.2 距离和静立占位   11
2.3 执裁防守   13
2.4 观察比赛情况的始末   15
2.5 选位、开角（45°）和调整   17
2.6 赛前会及 FIBA iRef PG App 的使用   19
2.7 做出宣判、决策和沟通   23
2.8 手势和报告   27
2.9 跳球 / 执行裁判（抛球）   33
2.10 跳球 / 非执行裁判   35
2.11 观察一次投篮情况（保护投篮队员）   35
2.12 掷球入界的管理（一般情况和前场端线）   37
2.13 骗取犯规   39
2.14 比赛和进攻计时钟的掌控   45

第 3 章

3. 手势和术语   53
3.1 官方裁判员手势   53
3.2 篮球裁判基本术语   71

国际篮联裁判员手册
个人执裁技术
（英文版）

第1章 GENERAL 通则

CHAPTER 1

1. GENERAL

1.1 BASKETBALL OFFICIATING

Generally, sports officiating is challenging and more so in the game of basketball – especially where ten athletic players are moving fast in a restricted area. Naturally the game has changed and the court has actually become larger, not in actual court size but in the playing and refereeing sense. Play situations are spread all over the court with every player able to play in almost every position. Naturally this sets a new requirement for basketball refereeing. It is good to remember that improving daily should not be considered as actual progress but rather is only designed to keep pace with the game's development – this is called evolution and this will occur regardless if we want it or not.

Sometimes there is a tendency to define basketball officiating as a very complex combination of various skills. It is true it requires many abilities by the referee, but the bottom line is that all these skills aim to achieve one thing - being ready to referee the play or handle situations that may arise during the game. All the training should focus on game preparation to assist referees to address various situations in games.

Refereeing is:
Anticipate what will happen — Active mind-set
Understand what is happening — Basketball knowledge
React properly for what has happened — Mental Image Training

1.2 IMAGE OF AN ELITE BASKETBALL REFEREE

FIBA has one golden rule when it comes to prioritising for referee training for FIBA games -Game Control. That is ensuring a smooth running and dynamic game where players are able to showcase their basketball skills. This is the image FIBA is looking for. The two or three appointed referees are the ones who are responsible for this game control.

第1章

1. 通则

1.1 篮球比赛执裁

一般而言，执裁体育比赛是十分具有挑战性的，在篮球比赛中更是如此——特别是当 10 名运动员在有限的空间范围内快速移动时。自然而然地，比赛就发生了很多变化，比赛场地实际上变大了。这不是篮球场的实际大小发生变化，而是对比赛和执裁的意义上而言的。对抗的情况遍布全场，每个队员几乎都能在任何位置上进行比赛。自然，这为篮球裁判的工作提出了新的要求。最好记住，日常业务改进和提高难以被称为业务能力的进步，而只是作为跟上篮球运动发展节奏的必备条件。这就是所谓的进步，并且无论我们同意与否，都会发生这种改变。

有这样一种趋势，将执裁篮球比赛定义为一项包含多种不同复杂技能的综合体。确实，它需要裁判员具备多项能力。但底线是，所有技能都旨在达成一个目标，准备好执裁比赛或处理好比赛中可能出现的情况。

执裁是：

预测场上将要发生什么——动态思维
理解场上正在发生什么——篮球知识
恰当反映已经发生什么——心理训练

1.2 精英篮球裁判员的形象

在国际篮联的裁判员培训中心有一项优先进行的培训内容，也就是国际篮联的黄金法则——比赛控制。目的是为了确保比赛能够流畅顺利且具有活力地进行，以便让运动员能够充分展示自己的篮球技能，这是国际篮联希望发生的情况。归根结底，裁判员要对比赛负责。

It is good to define and remember that game control is different to game management. Ultimately, it is the Referees that are in charge of the game. They define what is allowed and what is not – nobody else.

Having said that, it is equally important that referees look and act like they are in charge. Referees should give a non-verbal message that they are ready and able to make decisions. The core function of refereeing is decision making. Referees need to feel comfortable in making decisions without hesitation in the decision making process. Of course, the correctness of these decisions can be analysed after the event and so referees must demonstrate confidence and trust or at the very least present so that others view them this way (perception).

Therefore, FIBA has added the topic of "court presence" to its training program. It includes mental training with an "I am in charge" concept. This will be combined with a physical training plan to create an image of a strong and athletic body, fitting into the image of professionalism and promoting game control.

"Controlling is an attitude"

记住控制比赛和管理比赛是不同的。最终，裁判员要对比赛负责——绝不是其他人。他们定义什么是允许的，什么是不被允许的。

　　行文至此，裁判员的形象和举止也是同样重要的。裁判员应当以非语言的信号来表现出自己已经做好准备并且能够很好地执裁比赛。执裁的核心要义是决策。裁判员需要在决策过程中毫不犹豫地做出决定。当然，这些决定的正确与否可以在赛后进行分析总结。因此，裁判员必须表现出自信和信任，或者至少是在当下，让其他人看起来他们是这样的。

　　因此，国际篮联在训练计划中增加了"赛场仪容仪表"的课题。它包含了以"我在执裁"为核心的心理表象训练内容。这将与体能训练计划相结合，打造一个强壮的运动型身体形象，以适应专业形象并提升对比赛的控制。

"控制是一种态度"

第 2 章
INDIVIDUAL OFFICIATING TECHNIQUES (IOT)
个人执裁技术

CHAPTER 2

2. INDIVIDUAL OFFICIATING TECHNIQUES (IOT)

2.1 INTRODUCTION

Individual Officiating Techniques (IOT) is the most important foundation for either 2 Person Officiating (2PO) or 3 Person Officiating (3PO). It is evident that in the past 15 years there has been a heavy focus on 3PO (namely for the mechanical movements of the referees on the floor). This has led to a lack of knowledge in how to actually referee individual play phases in the game – this being the fundamental skills that referees need to possess in order to process and facilitate the correct decision. These are inherent skills of IOT and are similarly relevant to both 2PO and 3PO.

In analysing play phases and calling the game, some basic principles are necessary to follow :	
Have proper distance from the play – keeping an open ang leand remaining stationary. Do not move too close to the play and narrow your field of vision.	**Distance & Stationary**
The priority of the referee in an on ball competitive match-up is to focus the attention on the illegality of the defensive player whilstkeeping the offensive ball handler in your field of vision.	**Referee the defence**
Always look for illegal actions to call.	**Active mind-set**
Have the key players (1on1) or as many players as possible in yourfield of vision in order to see any illegal action.	**45° and Open angle**
Understand when the play has ended so you can move to the next play –mentally / physically.	**Stay with the play until it is over**

第 2 章

2. 个人执裁技术（IOT）

2.1 引言

个人执裁技术无论对 2 人执裁还是 3 人执裁来说都是最重要的。显而易见的是，在过去的 15 年里 3 人执裁更加受到重视（即裁判员在球场上根据裁判法移动），这导致了裁判员缺乏相关知识——如何在一场比赛中执裁各种不同的情况——这是裁判员需要具备的基本技能，以提高正确的宣判率。这些都是个人执裁技术的必要技能，对 2 人执裁和 3 人执裁都适用。

在分析比赛和宣判的时侯，遵循以下基本原则是十分必要的：	
与队员保持适当的距离——保持开角并保持静立占位。不要太靠近队员，这样会缩小你的视野。	距离和静立占位
执裁有球的情况时，最重要的是注意观察防守队员的动作合法性，同时视野不离开持球的进攻队员。	执裁防守
积极寻找非法行为来鸣哨。	动态思维
为了能看到所有的非法行为，将关键队员（1 对 1）或尽可能多的队员置于你的视野里。	45° 和开角
了解一次攻防矛盾何时结束，你才可以去关注下一对攻防矛盾——心理上／身体上。	注意力保持在一次攻防矛盾上，直到它结束

The lack of adhering to the above mentioned principles are the main reasons for wrong decisions being made on the floor. Simple as that!

When referees are able to have proper primary coverage for all obvious plays, it will substantially increase the quality of refereeing. These obvious plays, if missed, are the determining factors in peoples' mind as to what constitutes an acceptable level of officiating.

"Primary Coverage in Obvious Plays"

2.2 DISTANCE & STATIONARY

Target: To identify and understand the key points and impact of maintaining a proper distance from the play and being stationary when refereeing competitive match ups.

Many referees have the tendency to think that moving up and down the court and being very close to the play helps them to make correct decisions.

Therefore, we need to understand and focus on these two main issues:

1. **Distance -** When refereeing the play, it is important to maintain an appropriate distance from the play, without getting too close. The referee can lose perspective, as all movements appear to look faster. Imagine yourself watching the game from the upper deck of the stand and you will see that the players' movements look slower than at the court level. They only appear to look that way, but obviously they are not.

2. **Stationary -** Often referees that are engaged with the play are not conscious as to whether they are moving or not when the action starts. It is common sense that if we want to focus on something it is best to do so whilst stationary. These same two principles apply to refereeing.

If a referee has the proper distance from the play (3-6 meters):

  a. The possibility of an emotional or reaction call decreases.

  b. He can maintain a perspective as movements look slower.

没有遵守上述原则是造成裁判宣判失误的主要原因。就这么简单！

当裁判员的主要视角可以完全覆盖所有明显的矛盾和对抗时，这将会大大提高宣判质量。如果对这些明显的矛盾与对抗没有及时做出宣判，就会影响人们对执裁水平的认可程度。

> **"在主责任区域覆盖明显的比赛情况"**

2.2 距离和静立占位

目标：明确和理解执裁激烈对抗时和队员保持适当距离以及保持静立占位的关键点和重要影响。

许多裁判员都认为在球场上快速移动以及靠近比赛能帮助他们做出正确的宣判。

因此，我们需要了解和关注两个主要问题。

1. **距离**：执裁时保持适当距离的重要性。距离太近，裁判员会失去一些视角，所以有些动作看起来就会很快。想象一下，你从看台的上面观看比赛，你会发现队员的动作看起来比球场上的动作要慢。他们只是看起来是这样，但很显然他们并不慢。

2. **静立占位**：通常专注于比赛的裁判员意识不到他们自己是否在移动。有一种常识是，如果我们想专注于什么事情的话，那最好是保持静态。这两条原则同样适用于执裁。

如果裁判员距离队员有适当的距离（3～6米）：

a. 情绪宣判或反应宣判的可能性减少。

b. 裁判员可以保持一个视角，让动作看起来更慢一些。

c. He can maintain a wide angle, which increases the possibility of seeing more players in the field of vision.

d. He is able to see the big picture (next plays to follow, control the clocks, identify where partners)

If a referee is stationary when he is making a judgment:

a. His eyes are not bouncing and concentration increases

b. A correct decision is more likely due to being focused and concentrated.

It is important that a referee must move to be in the right position to see the gap (this is different than position adjustment); and must do so as quickly as possible. Stop, Observe and Decide.

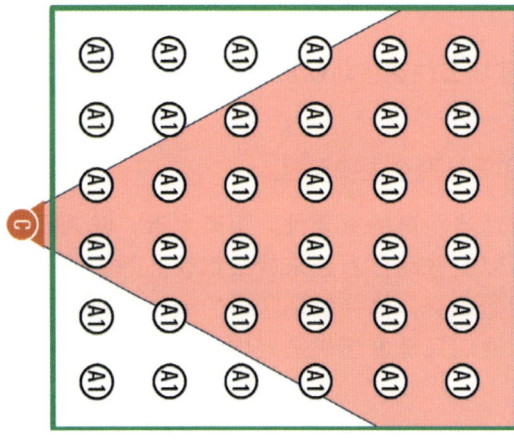

Diagram 1:
Proper distance creates wider angle and the referee is able to have more players in his field of vision at the same time. Example in the first row 2 players, second row 3 players, third row 4 players, etc. Totally 26 players out of 36 (72%).

2.3 REFEREEING THE DEFENCE

Target: To identify the primary focus when analysing a 1 on 1 play.

The concept of refereeing the defence is one of the corner stones for accurate basketball refereeing. Essentially, it means that the priority of the referee in an on ball competitive match-up is to focus the attention on the illegality of the defensive player whilst keeping the offensive ball handler in your field of vision. The referee is required to get into a position that allows them to clearly see the defensive player.

c. 裁判员可以保持一个开阔的视角，这增加了在视野中可以看到更多队员的可能性。

d. 裁判员能够看到大局（跟随队员，控制时钟，确定其他裁判员的位置）。

如果裁判员在静立状态中做出判断：

a. 他的视线是固定的，注意力更加集中。

b. 更加集中和专注的注意力，将增加正确判断的可能性。

重要的是，裁判员必须移动到合适的位置去看缝隙（这不同于调整位置）；必须尽快做到这一点。停止，观察然后判断。

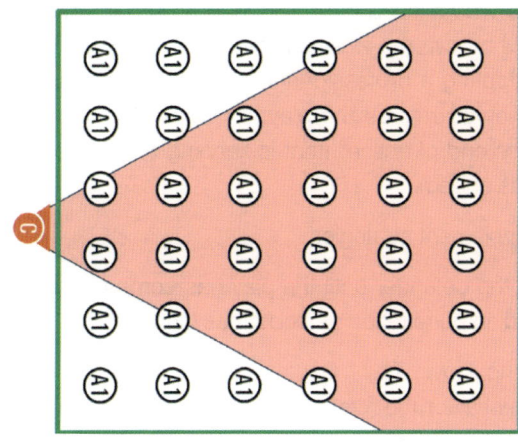

图1：
适当的距离可以创造更好的观察角度，裁判员在同一时间可以在他的视野里看到更多的队员。例如，第一排2名队员，第二排3名队员，第三排4名队员……36名队员中共有26个队员（72%）

2.3 执裁防守

目标：分析1对1时的主要注意事项和重点。

执裁防守的工作是篮球精准执裁的基石之一。从本质上讲，这意味在观察比赛中有球对位攻防时优先将注意力集中在防守队员是否正当防守上，同时保持进攻队员在你的视野中。裁判员必须站在一个能让他们清楚看到防守队员的位置上。

Note: We are not refereeing the space between the players, we are refereeing the defence itself - but you need to have a position where you see the space between players in order to referee the defence.

When refereeing on ball focus your attention on the illegality of the defensive player!

2.4 STAY WITH THE PLAY

Target: To understand how to increase quality control in play situations.

On occasions, referees miss an obvious foul. Unfortunately, it often looks like the only persons in the arena who missed the obvious foul were the two or three persons on the court who have the whistle. The key to correctly calling these obvious plays is by adopting a professional discipline – that is to be patient and careful every time you referee the play. It is expected referees will "stay with the play until the end of action" (that is keeping your eyes and attention on the play until it has ended).

Practically, referees need to implement strategies:

   a. mentally focussing on the defender until the play has come to its end e.g. shooter has landed, in penetration defender has landed.

   b. physically do not start to move. Trail / Centre stepping backwards on the shot – has the potential for the referee to mentally release the play before ball has entered the basket or the defensive team has gained control of the rebound.

Processing the play (Patient Whistle)

Before blowing their whistle referees should process the entire play from the start - through the development - until the end before making a call. This will produce more analytical decision instead of only seeing the end of the play and reacting to it (emotional decision).

注意：我们不需要在意队员之间的距离，我们需要执裁防守动作本身，但你需要有一个可以观察队员之间的空间的位置以更好地执裁防守。

> **当执裁有球攻防的时候，将注意力集中在防守队员动作的非法行为上！**

2.4 观察比赛情况的始末

目标：了解如何提高对不同的比赛情况的控制能力。

有时候，裁判员也会有很明显的漏判。不幸的是，整个球馆内漏掉了那个明显犯规的人正是场上执哨的那两三个人。对这些明显的情况能做出正确吹判的关键就是接受一个专业准则——那就是你对每一次吹罚都需要保持耐心和谨慎，这要求裁判"观察比赛情况的全过程，直到其结束"（这是要求你将目光和注意力放在比赛情况本身，直到比赛情况的结束）。

实际上，裁判员需要实施一些策略：

a. 保持对防守队员的全神贯注，直到攻守情况结束，例如投篮队员已经落地，在突破时防守队员已经落地。

b. 身体上不要移动。追踪/中央裁判在投篮情况时后撤——在球进入球篮或防守方控制篮板球之前，裁判员有可能从精神上出现了松懈。

解析比赛情况（耐心哨）

裁判员在鸣哨之前应当解析完整的比赛情况，从开始到发展，直到结束才判断是否做出宣判。相对于仅仅通过比赛情况的结尾做出反应（情绪化的决定），"耐心哨"则更具理性。

2.5 POSITIONING, OPEN ANGLE (45°) AND ADJUSTMENTS

Target: To understand the impact and technique of maximising the number of the players within your field of vision at all times.

It has been stated that referees must always look for illegal actions (something to call). Logically, if a referee has more players in his field of vision, the chances of seeing illegal actions dramatically increase. Namely, those referees who have positioned themselves on the court with proper distance and a wide open angle, are more likely to have a higher level of accuracy thus leading to a higher standard of performance.

Analysis proves that the concept of maintaining an open angle is not necessarily well understood by referees. Often referees who have established an open angle, unnecessarily move again, losing the open angle and becoming straight lined on the play.

A second key principle is to have both Lead (L) and Trail (T) on the edge of the play (players and ball).This way referees are able to maintain as many players as possible in their field of vision. As a result,it is important for Lead to move on the baseline with ball (mirroring the ball) and for Trail to always be behind the play (between the last player and basket in the backcourt). The following diagram demonstrates the advantage of being at the "edge of the play" and having a 45° angle).

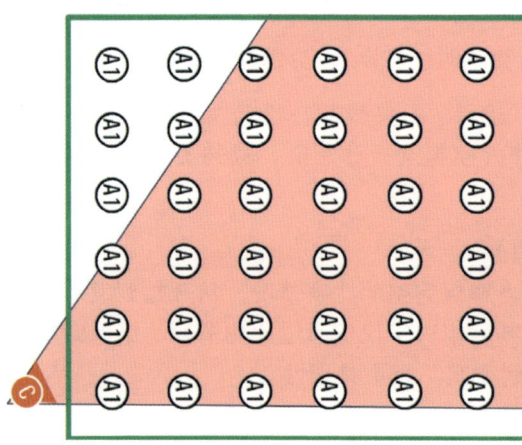

Diagram 2:
It is important to find a position and angle on the court where the referee is able to observe as many players as possible. If you compare the number of the players covered with Diagram 2, you will find that with 45° and an "edge of the play" adjustment, a total of 32 players out of 36(89%) are covered at the same time.

2.5 选位、开角（45°）和调整

目标：认识到使你视野中的队员数量最大化的影响和技巧。

如前所述，裁判员必须不停地寻找非法的行为（需要判罚的行为）。从逻辑上讲，如果一个裁判员在视野内能看到更多的队员，那他看到非法行为的机会将大大增加。也就是说，能保持适当的距离和开阔的视野的裁判员越有可能提高其执法水平，从而做出更高水准的表现。

分析证明，维持开角的观念并没有被裁判员很好地理解。通常已经建立了很好的开角的裁判员由于一些不必要的移动而失去了开角，从而直接影响了对比赛的判断。

第二个关键原则是前导裁判（L）和追踪裁判（T）位于比赛的同一侧（队员和球）。这样裁判能够将尽可能多的队员置于其视野之中。因此，对于前导裁判来说，在端线跟随球的移动就变得非常重要（映射球），而对于追踪裁判来说最重要的是保持在比赛的最后方（在后场的最后一个队员和篮板之间）。下面的图演示了在"比赛边缘"和具备 45°角的优势。

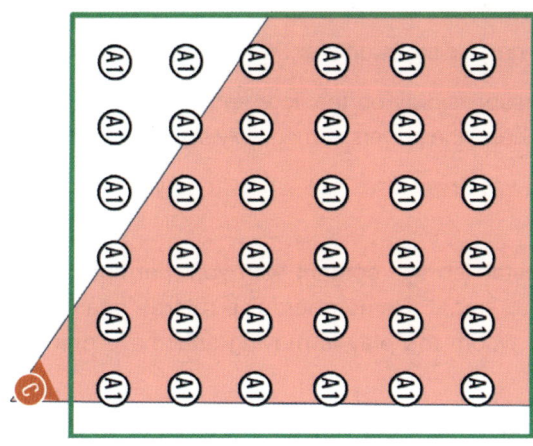

图 2：
重要的是在球场上找到一个能够观察到尽可能多的队员的位置和角度。如果比较图 2 中覆盖的队员的数量，你会发现 45° 和"比赛边缘"在同一时间覆盖了 36 名队员中的 32 名（89%）。

The principles for positioning and open angle are:

   a. Move to the right spot and establish the open angle.
   b. Anticipate (mentally one step ahead of the play) where you need to be.
   c. Adjust to the play to maintain the open angle (step here, step there).
   d. Always move with a purpose, know where you need to go and why.
   e. Go where ever you need to go to be in the position to referee the play (different to the Working Area).
   f. If the initial position is correct – there is a less need to move, but do not be STATIC (you need to adjust all the time according to the play and players' movement).

2.6 PRE-GAME CONFERENCE AND USE OF FIBA IREF PG APP

Target: To know the topics that have to be covered during the pre-game conference and what functionalities are offered by the App.

A pre-game conference is absolutely necessary. The concept is to ensure you and your partner(s) are on the same page when officiating together. This promotes good teamwork and good officiating.

Some general topics for pre-game discussion are:

1. Know your areas of responsibility on the floor and avoid having both referees watch the ball and the players immediately surrounding it.
2. Referee the play away from the ball when it is your primary responsibility.
3. With double calls, establish eye contact with your partner before proceeding with your signal. Remember: The referee nearest to the play or towards whom the play is moving shall have primary responsibility.
4. Give help when required on out-of-bounds situations, but only when requested to do so by your partner. Get into the habit of establishing eye contact.

选位和开角的原则是：

a. 移动到正确的位置并建立开角。

b. 必要的时候进行预判（从思想上领先比赛一步）并去你将要去的地方。

c. 根据比赛进行调整以保持开角（移步到这里，移步到那里）。

d. 始终有目的地移动，知道要去哪、为什么。

e. 去任何你需要去的位置来执裁比赛（不同于分工区域）。

f. 如果初始位置是正确的，则不需要移动，但不要完全静止不动（你需要根据比赛情况和队员的移动来做调整）。

2.6 赛前会及 FIBA iRef PG App 的使用

目标：了解赛前会期间必须涵盖的主题以及应用程序提供的功能。

赛前会是绝对有必要的。讨论内容是为了确保你和你的同伴在执裁过程中统一。这可以提升团队合作精神和优秀执裁习惯。

一些赛前会的常规话题：

1. 知道你在场上不同区域的责任，并避免在双方队员迅速移动的过程中有两名裁判员同时看球。

2. 当无球区是自己的主责时，确保观察无球区的攻防矛盾。

3. 出现双哨时，打出手势之前与你的同伴建立目光联系。记住，离比赛情况最近或正对迎面而来比赛情况的裁判员应负主责。

4. 仅当你的同伴在界外球情况中请求帮助时给予帮助。养成建立目光联系的习惯。

5. Try to know at all times, not only where the ball and all the players are located, but also the location of your partner.

6. In fast break situations, especially where the offensive players outnumber those on defence, let the nearest referee make the decision on whether or not to call the foul. Avoid the temptation to make a call when you are ten (10) metres or more away from the action.

7. Blow your whistle for a foul only when it has an effect on the action. Incidental–marginal contact should be ignored.

8. Establish your standards early in the game. The game will become easier to control. Rough and over-aggressive play must always be penalized. The players will adjust to the way you allow them to play.

9. Try to maintain the best possible position and a wide angle of vision between the defensive and offensive players. Be on top of the play having proper distance and being stationary when you make the decision (call or no call).

To help the referees in this matter, FIBA has developed an FIBA iRef Pre-Game App that can be easily used everywhere to help the referee crew to prepare for the game.

You can download the application from Apple App Store or Google Play Store.

5. 争取始终都知道球和所有队员的位置,以及你同伴的位置。

6. 在快攻情况中,尤其是进攻队员多于防守队员时,应当让最近的裁判员判断是否做出宣判。要避免自己出现在 10 米开外或是较远的地方做出宣判。

7. 只有当一次接触影响了比赛情况时才鸣哨。我们应忽略附带接触。

8. 在比赛的早期建立尺度,比赛便会变得更容易把控。粗暴和过分动作的情况必须被判罚。队员们会根据裁判员的尺度自我调整。

9. 要在攻防队员之间争取获得最佳占位和最宽阔的视野。要擅长在做出判断时(宣判或不宣判)保持距离和静立占位。

为了在这个问题上帮助裁判员,国际篮联开发了可在任何地方轻松操作的 FIBA iRef Pre-Game App 以帮助裁判员们做好赛前准备。

你可以从苹果应用商店或谷歌应用商店下载。

2.7 MAKING A CALL, DECISION MAKING AND COMMUNICATION

Target: To know how to make the call and being able to immediately communicate the decision verbally and with standard hand signals.

Sometimes we underestimate the value of simple basic techniques in creating the solid foundations of successful basketball officiating at the top level.

When blowing the pea-less whistle, it is important to have enough air (force) in a short period to enter into whistle. This creates the strong decisive sound. Given the need to communicate verbally the decision after making the call, it is imperative we retain some air in our lungs.

Therefore following key points are important:

1. Technique how to blow the whistle – strong short blow ("spit") into the whistle - one time.
2. Release the whistle out of the mouth after making a call.
3. Indicating the relevant signals for the decision.
4. Support your decision verbally "Foul blue 5, offensive foul; Travelling etc…"
5. Less is more – remember less and once you indicate/state something, the power of the message is stronger (practice the key words and how to articulate them clearly).

2.7.1 MAKING A 'NO-CALL'

Referees are to use official signals only. Where a referee is making a decision on a play and a no call situation eventuates, referees are not to demonstrate or use other signals for the 'no call'. This is particularly relevant in such situations where your partner sees an illegal action on the same play due to having a different angle and actually makes a call.

2.7.2 MAKING AN OUT-OF-BOUNDS CALL

When calling out-of-bounds plays, referee should always support their decision verbally i.e. saying "blue ball" at the same time as showing the direction. This will be very useful if you accidentally point in the wrong direction.

2.7 做出宣判、决策和沟通

目标：知道如何去鸣哨，以及能够针对决定及时地通过口语和标准手势进行联系。

有时我们低估了一些最简单、最基本技术的价值，这些基本技术能在高水平的篮球比赛中为裁判员的正确判罚打下坚实的基础。

当要吹响口哨时，能在很短促的时间内将足够多的空气吹入口哨是非常重要的，这可以使哨声听起来更响亮、更果断。如果需要在鸣哨后对判罚进行一些口头沟通，那么我们就必须在肺部保留一些空气。

因此，以下要点十分重要：

1. 鸣哨的技巧——短促有力地将空气吹入口哨——鸣一声。
2. 鸣哨之后就把口哨吐出来。
3. 展示相关判罚的手势。
4. 口头说出你的判决："蓝队 5 号，进攻犯规；走步……"
5. 少即是多——当指出/陈述某样东西，少且只说一遍会让你传达的信息更有力度（练习关键词以及如何清晰地表达它们）。

2.7.1 做出"不宣判"的决定

裁判员只可以使用国际篮联官方手势。当裁判员对一个比赛情况不做出宣判的决定时，裁判员不能使用任何手势。这一点非常重要，尤其是当一位处于不同占位的同伴对同一个比赛情况观察到非法情况并做出了宣判。

2.7.2 宣判一次球出界

在宣判球出界时裁判员应始终用口语支持他们的宣判，比如：在指出方向的同时喊出"蓝队的球"。如果你无意中指错方向，这一点便十分实用了。

2.7.3 MAKING A FOUL CALL

It is important to communicate your decision to players and other participants clearly and quickly. In act of shooting situations people are eager to know whether there will be free throws or not. To avoid confusion in these situations referees should communicate their decision immediately by using appropriate authorized signal.

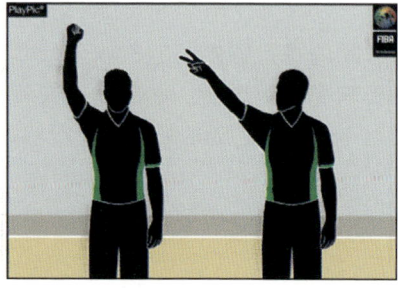
Foul in Act of Shooting (FAOS)

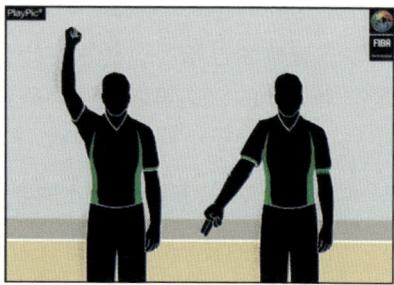
Foul not in Act of Shooting (FNAOS)

Note: These signals should only be used when there is an act of shooting situation or potential act of shooting situation.

Unsportsmanlike foul – 0-1-2 technique

When calling a situation with a potential UF action, the following protocols should be used:

0. Make the decision to call something

1. Indicate foul signal first (gives time to process what criteria is used for UF)

2. Upgrade the signal for UF Referees should avoid showing the UF hand signal directly when calling a foul.

0.

1.

2.

2.7.3 宣判一次犯规

将你的宣判清晰快速地传达给队员们和观众们很重要。在投篮动作的情况中大家都迫切想知道是否会给予罚球机会。为了避免在这些情况中发生误会,裁判员应快速打出正式手势传达给大家。

对投篮动作的犯规

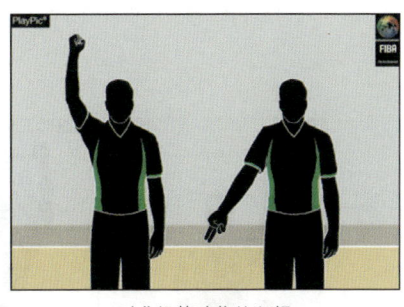
对非投篮动作的犯规

注:这些手势仅仅应在有或可能有投篮动作出现的情况中使用。

违反体育运动精神的犯规——0-1-2 技术

当宣判一起可能是违反体育运动精神的犯规的情况时,应遵循以下步骤:

0. 对所见情况做出决定和宣判。

1. 先打出犯规手势(给予自己时间以判断符合违反体育运动精神的犯规的哪一条标准)。

2. 将手势升级为违反体育运动精神的犯规。裁判员应避免在宣判犯规时直接打出违反体育运动精神的犯规手势。

0.

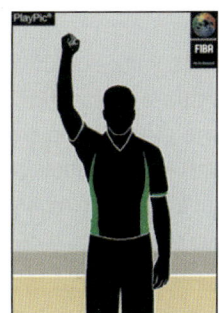
1.

2.

3point shot, foul & basket

When calling a defensive foul in the shot; the following protocol is to be used:

1. Shot is taken – 3 Point Attempt Signal
2. Foul is called – switch to Regular Foul Signal (use the same hand)
3. The ball goes to into basket – Successful 3 Point Signal

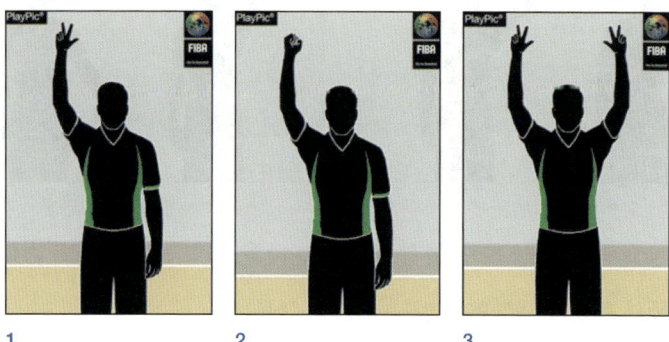

1.   2.   3.

2.8 SIGNALS & REPORTING

Target: To identify the different phases and techniques of having strong and decisive signals as part of court presence.

Referees should use only the official signals defined in the FIBA Basketball Rules. It is a professional sign and attitude to use only the official signals. Personal habits and preferences only demonstrate a lack of understanding and professional attitude.

When communicating decisions with signals, it is good to remember that the use of signals creates a strong perception among the people who are watching the referees. It is one piece in the overall package of providing a trusted and accepted refereeing image. Often we think that there is no need to practise the official signals at all, but it is highly necessary.

3 分球、犯规和球中篮

在投篮期间宣判一起防守犯规时,应遵循以下步骤:

1. 已投篮——打出 3 分试投手势。
2. 宣判犯规——转变为普通犯规手势(使用同一只手)。
3. 球中篮——打出 3 分投篮成功手势。

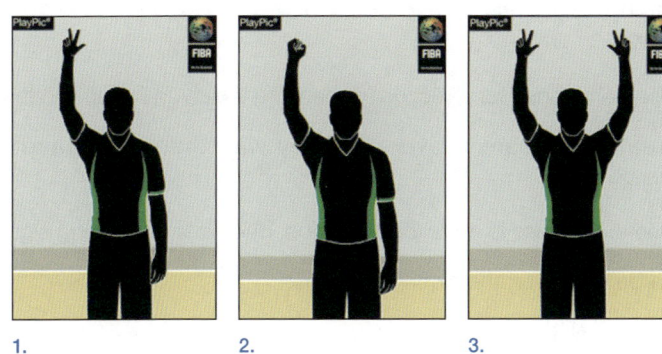

1. 2. 3.

2.8 手势和报告

目标:作为球场气质风度的一部分,应当明确知晓做出有力、果断的手势的不同步骤和各种技术。

裁判员只能使用国际篮联篮球规则中定义的官方手势。只使用官方手势是一种专业的标志和态度。个人习惯和偏好只会表现为缺乏理解和缺乏专业态度。

要记住在用手势传达判罚决定时,手势会给所有看裁判员的人产生直观印象。它是展示可靠和可被接受的裁判员良好形象的一个方面。通常我们都认为根本不需要练习官方手势,但这是非常有必要的。

A checklist for successful use of the signals:

1. Use official and authorized FIBA signals.
2. Rhythm
   a. Each signal has a start and a stop.
   b. When finishing the signal, freeze it and count "one-two" in your mind.
3. Strong, Sharp, Visible and Decisive signals (practice this in front of the mirror).
4. Use both hands for direction, depending which shoulder is in the front.
5. Treat each team, player and play with the same standard (no histrionics).
6. Remember less is more (no repetition, one clear and strong signal).
7. Verbally support the signal at all times.

2.8.1 REPORTING

A checklist for successful reporting to the scorers' table:

1. Walk sharply to a spot where you have visual contact with the table. Minimize distance – think where is your next position after reporting.
2. Stop, both feet side by side on the floor and breathe (body balance – shoulders level).
3. Rhythm (start - stop -"one - two" / start - stop-"one -two"/ start -stop- "one - two").
4. Identify: Number, nature of foul and penalty (throw-in or free throws).
5. Nature of the foul must be the same as what really happened in the play.
6. Verbally support the reporting to the scorer's table.

成功使用手势的列表：

1. 使用国际篮联官方许可的手势。

2. 节奏：

    a. 每个手势都有一个开始和停止。

    b. 当打出一个手势后，固定它，并在你的脑海里默念"一、二"。

3. 有力、干脆、清晰和果断的手势（可在镜子前练习）。

4. 会用双手来指方向，取决于哪个肩膀在比赛进攻的前方。

5. 对待每一个球队、队员和比赛采用相同的标准（不装腔作势）。

6. 记得少便是多（不要重复，一个明确而强烈的信号即可）。

7. 随时用口语解释手势。

2.8.1 报告

向记录台成功报告的列表：

1. 快步走到可与记录台建立目光联系的位置。减少移动距离并考虑到报告后要去的下一个位置。

2. 停止，双脚在地板上站稳和平稳地呼吸（身体平衡，肩膀挺直）。

3. 节奏（开始—停止"一、二"/开始—停止"一、二"/开始—停止"一、二"）。

4. 确定：号码、犯规性质和罚则（掷球入界或罚球）。

5. 犯规的性质必须和比赛中真实发生的情况一样。

6. 用语言支持向记录台的报告。

Foul with throw-in	Foul with free throws

1. Number	– No. 6	1. Number	– No. 6
2. Nature of foul	– Blocking foul	2. Nature of foul	– Illegal contact to hand
3. Penalty	– Throw-in direction	3. Penalty	– 2 free throws

Double Foul

1. Point to team A's bench and report the number
2. Point to team B's bench and report the number
3. Show how the game will continue

   3a. throw-in direction OR

   3b. jump ball situation & throw-in direction

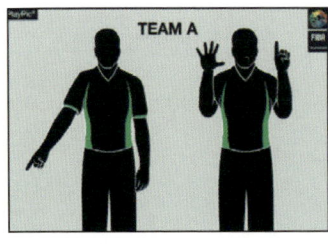

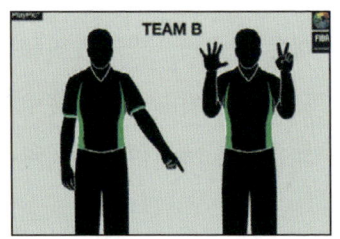

1.   2.

后续掷球入界的犯规	后续罚球的犯规

1. 号码 ——6号	1. 号码 ——6号
2. 犯规性质 —— 阻挡犯规	2. 犯规性质 —— 非法用手犯规
3. 罚则 —— 掷球入界的方向	3. 罚则 ——2次罚球

双方犯规

1. 指向 A 队球队席并报告号码

2. 指向 B 队球队席并报告号码

3. 显示继续比赛的方式

    3a. 掷球入界的方向，或者

    3b. 跳球情况以及掷球入界的方向

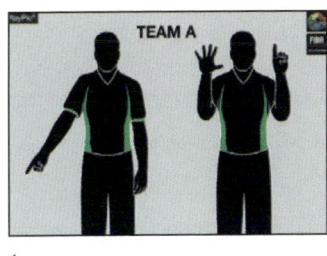

1.

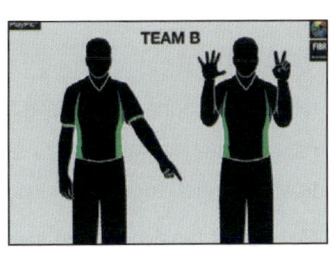

2.

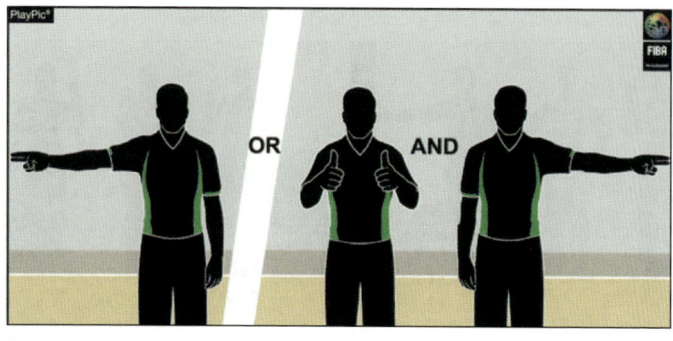

3a.   3b.

2.9 JUMP BALL / ACTIVE REFEREE (TOSSING THE BALL)

Target: *To identify the different phases and correct techniques during the ball toss.*

Jump-ball situations are exciting, but unfortunately sometimes the administrating referee is unable to toss the ball properly. Analysis indicates that 50% of the violations during the jump-ball are caused by a poor toss by the referee. In other words, they could have been avoided. Tossing the ball is something that needs to be trained on a regular basis, unlike what is currently the case.

It is crucial to understand that the jumpers are tense and will react easily on any movement caused by the referee. So therefore it is crucial to avoid any unnecessary movements.

A checklist for a successful ball toss:

    a. Players are tense - avoid any extra movements.

    b. Style of tossing the ball is irrelevant (two hands - low or high, one hand - low or high).

    c. It is more important is to have one solid upward movement to toss the ball

    d. Level of the ball at the start – the lower the ball is – the longer it has to travel to reach the "highest point".

    e. Speed & intensiveness of the toss (lower starting point – more intensive and faster).

    f. No whistle in the mouth when administrating the toss.

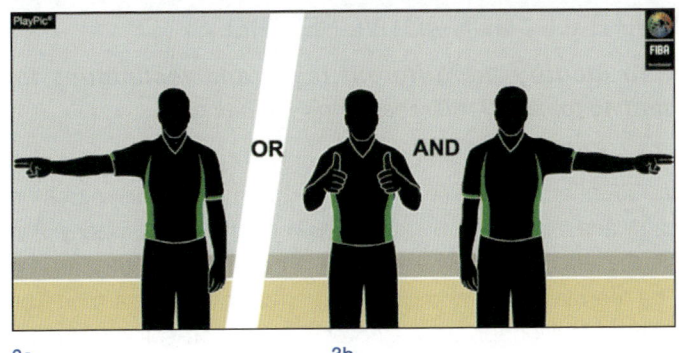

3a.　　　　　　　　3b.

2.9 跳球 / 执行裁判（抛球）

目标：在掷球时确定不同的站位和抛球的正确方式。

跳球的情况是令人兴奋的，但不幸的是有时执行裁判不能正确地抛球。分析表明，在比赛中 50% 的违例行为是由裁判员抛球不当造成的。换句话说，他们本来可以避免的。抛球是需要经常训练的东西，而不是像现在这样。

重要是要明白，跳球队员是紧张的，并会很容易对裁判员所引起的任何动作做出反应。因此，避免任何不必要的动作是至关重要的。

成功抛球的要领：

a. 队员很紧张，裁判要避免做任何额外的动作。

b. 抛球的方式是自由的（两只手抛球或低或高，一只手抛球或低或高）。

c. 更重要的是要有一个向上运动的姿势来抛球。

d. 开始抛球时球的水平高度——球越低，到达"最高点"所需的时间越长。

e. 抛球的速度和力度（较低的抛球起点——更集中和更快）。

f. 进行抛球时口中不要含口哨。

2.10 JUMP BALL / NON-ACTIVE REFEREE(S)

Target: To identify the different tasks and techniques for non-administrating (passive) referees during the ball toss.

The non-administrating referee(s) have only very limited duties during the jump-ball situations. Even so, from time to time we still witness obvious violations or administrating error(s) that are not officiated properly. A possible reason is that the non-active referee(s) is not ready to react to any illegal actions by the players or administrating errors by their partner. The active mind-set is the key for appropriate coverage. The non-active referee(s) should remind themselves (self talking) to identify illegal actions and the proper procedures that follow in case they take place.

A checklist for a successful coverage by non-active referee(s):

a. Call back the poor toss (too low, not straight, incorrect timing)

b. Call the violation if the ball is touched by jumpers on the way up (stealing the tap)

c. Call the violation if the non-jumpers are not staying outside the circle until ball is tapped legally by the jumper(s).

d. Controlling the game clock (10:00) and the shot clock (24") – ensuring they are reset where a violation is called before the ball is legally tapped.

e. Ensuring that any throw-in as a result of a violation by the jumper is placed in the new front court, close to the mid court line.

f. Checking that the alternating possession arrow is set properly after one of the teams has established the first possession of a live ball.

2.11 COVERING A SHOT (PROTECT THE SHOOTER)

Target: To have full coverage on all act of shooting situations.

Referees should have full coverage on obvious situations in their primary. A shot is an obvious play – always! The correct way to referee a shooting situation is to use a 1-2-3 technique for shooting situations. When used properly this technique provides the details for possible foul or fake call. The action need to have contact to be illegal.

2.10 跳球 / 非执行裁判

目标：确认非执行裁判在抛球时的不同任务和技术。

在跳球情况中，非执行裁判的职责非常有限。即使如此，我们时不时会看到明显的违例和由于没有恰当判罚而引起的执行错误。一个可能的原因是，非执行裁判不准备对队员的任何非法行为或者同伴的管理失误做出反应。积极心态的建立是建立良好视野的关键。为防止犯规的发生，非执行裁判应提醒自己（自言自语）找出非法行为以及随后采取的适当程序。

非执行裁判成功判罚的列表：

a. 宣判质量不高的抛球（过低、不直、不合适的时机）。

b. 球在上升过程中被跳球队员触碰了，判罚了违例。

c. 非跳球队员在跳球队员合法拍击球之前就提前进入了中圈，判罚了违例。

d. 控制比赛计时钟（10 分钟）和进攻计时钟（24 秒）——确保球被合法拍击之前吹罚违例时两个计时钟是复位的。

e. 确保由于跳球队员违例而导致的任何掷球入界都在靠近中线的新的前场执行。

f. 在某队建立了第一次控制活球后检查交替拥有箭头是否被正确设置。

2.11 观察一次投篮情况（保护投篮队员）

目标：全面覆盖所有的投篮情况。

裁判员应全面覆盖其主责任区发生的明显情况。一次投篮永远是一次明显的情况！在投篮情况中裁判员正确的观察方法是采用 1–2–3 技术。这种技术的合理采用可以提供给裁判员潜在犯规或骗取犯规的细节内容。发生接触是发生非法接触的前提。

1-2-3 technique on shooting situations

a. Referee defense all the time.

b. Check the play in following order: 1. hands 2. body 3. feet (landing).

c. Stay with the play until shooter has returned to the floor.

d. Only then turn your attention to ball & rebounds.

Diagram 3:
The 1-2-3 technique covering act of shooting situations.

2.12 THROW-IN ADMINISTRATION (GENERAL & FRONTCOURT ENDLINE)

Target: To identify the standard phases and correct administration procedure for all throw-in situations.

The throw-in administration should be an automatic (muscle memory) procedure. If done every time and with the proper technique, the referee will always be ready physically and mentally to cover the various types of play situations than can occur with a throw-in action.

Check list for the general throw-in procedure as an administrating referee:

1. Always designate the throw-in spot.

2. Use preventative officiating eg. "on the spot", "stay" or "don't move".

投篮情况中的 1-2-3 技术：

a. 始终执裁防守。

b. 按顺序观察比赛情况：1. 手，2. 身体，3. 脚（落地）。

c. 投篮队员落地之前保持视线不离开。

d. 最后才将注意力转移到球和篮板球。

图 3：
覆盖投篮情况的 1-2-3 技术

2.12 掷球入界的管理（一般情况和前场端线）

目标：确认所有掷球入界情况下的标准步骤和正确的管理程序。

掷球入界的管理应该是一个自动的（肌肉记忆）步骤。每次都要用恰当的技术完成，裁判随时都要做好身体和精神上的准备，应对发球时可能出现的各种情况。

作为执行裁判时，掷球入界的常规步骤：

1. 总要指定掷球入界地点。

2. 用预防性的执裁指令，比如"站在这个点"，"停住"或"别动"。

37

3. Check the clocks.
4. Take and maintain distance from the play.
5. Put the whistle in your mouth while holding ball.
6. Bounce the ball to the player.
7. Start the visual count.
8. Observe the throw-in and action surrounding.
9. Use the start clock signal.

Note: When a throw-in is taken on the end line in the frontcourt, the active referee will blow the whistle before placing the ball at the player's disposal for the throw-in.

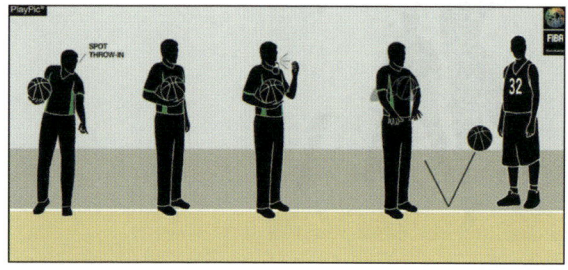

Diagram 4:
The different phases of the correct throw-in procedure for the administrating referee.

2.13 FAKE A FOUL

Target: To know what is a fake and how to manage the situation when it occurs.

Faking is behaviour that does not fit within the spirit of sportsmanship and fair play and for this reason, it is the referees who need to identify the action early and to clean it up early.

Faking is where a player pretends he has been fouled or makes theatrical exaggerated movements to create an opinion of being fouled and therefore gaining an unfair advantage. Note: A flop is a special type of the defender's action (charge/block) but it is still a fake. A fake without any contact with an opponent is considered to be excessive fake.

3. 核对计时钟。

4. 和比赛保持一定距离。

5. 持球的时候将哨子放到嘴里。

6. 将球击地传给队员。

7. 开始清楚可见的读秒。

8. 观察掷球入界和周围的情况。

9. 使用开表手势。

注意：在前场端线发球时，执行裁判在把球给队员掷球入界之前要鸣哨。

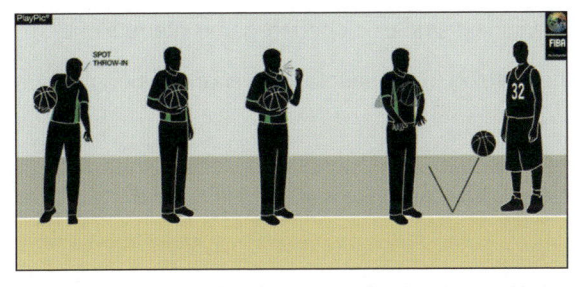

图 4：
执行裁判正确掷球入界步骤的不同阶段

2.13 骗取犯规

目标：知道什么是一次骗取犯规情况并清楚当其发生时如何处理。

骗取犯规是一种不符合体育运动精神和公平竞赛的行为，正因为如此，裁判员需要尽早识别和清除这类行为。

骗取犯规是一名队员为了假装被犯规或使用戏剧性的夸张动作来制造被犯规的假象而从中获取不正当利益。注：假摔是防守队员的一种特定行为（撞人/阻挡），但它依然是一种骗取犯规。与对手间不发生任何身体接触的骗取犯规被视为是严重的骗取犯规。

It is important for referees to know the game of basketball and the technical movements and tactics of the players to assist them in officiating faking, especially where players maximise the impact of marginal contact.

When a player is faking during the play the referees shall give a warning to the player and to the head coach. This serves as a warning for that team. Each team is entitled to one warning. Any repetition of faking by the same team is a technical foul.

An excessive fake results in a direct technical foul (no warning required).

1. Protocol for the standard fake warning during the play:

    a. A fake action by the player during the play (no stoppage).

    b. Show the "raise-the-lower arm" signal to indicate the "fake action".

    c. Verbal support – for example "white 8 fake".

2. Protocol for the warning(next stop clock period-game interruption):

    a. Communicate the warning to the affected player and the coach plus he co-referee(s).

    b. Show the "Raise-the-lower arm" signal and demonstrate the "Technical Foul" signal supported verbally.

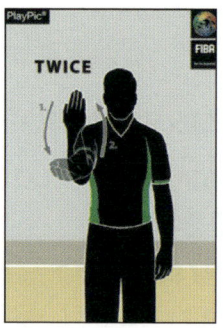 

3. On repetitive fake action or on excessive fake resulting in a technical foul, whistle with:

知晓篮球运动及其技战术对于裁判员来说非常重要，这能协助裁判员执裁骗取犯规情况，尤其是队员们在夸大附带的身体接触程度时。

比赛过程中队员出现骗取犯规情况时，裁判员应对该队员及其主教练提出警告。这次警告适用于全队。每队只有一次被警告机会。同队重复出现任何形式的骗取犯规都将导致一次技术犯规。

一次夸张的骗取犯规将直接导致一次技术犯规（无须警告）。

1. 比赛过程中对骗取犯规警告的标准方法：

    a. 比赛过程中出现队员骗取犯规的行为（未出现比赛停止）。

    b. 做出"前臂上抬两次"手势以表示发生了"骗取犯规行为"。

    c. 口语支持宣判——比如"白8骗取犯规"。

2. 警告程序（下一次比赛中断的停表期间）：

    a. 对违犯队员做出警告并传达给其教练员和裁判员同伴。

    b. 做出"前臂上抬两次"手势并结合口语做出"技术犯规"手势。

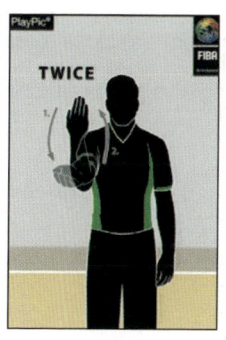

3. 重复出现骗取犯规行为或出现导致直接宣判技术犯规的夸张骗取犯规情况时，鸣哨，并：

a. Stop the clock signal.

b. "Raise-the-lower-arm" signal.

c. Followed by the "Technical Foul" signal.

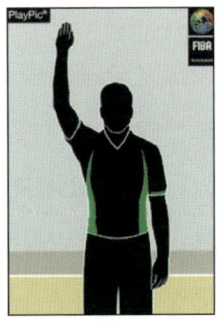 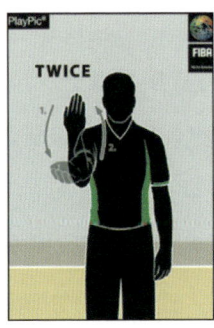 

Some signs of faking:
- Faker is looking for contact first (he needs a contact to make the fake).
- Head goes back (head fake) when contact does not occur on the head.
- Making theatrical, exaggerated movements.
- Jumping off spot and landing spot are close to each other.
- Feet go up in the air when falling and hands are prepared for the fall.

Not all the movements are fakes:
- If a dribbler extends his arm to create space – it is still an offensive foul in principle.
- If a player steps on another players foot and loses his balance – this is not a fake in principle.

It is important to see the entire play, not only the reaction of the player. Illegal contact is still to be called as a foul, marginal contacts are still part of the game and legal. If there is a foul on the play, there cannot be a fake on the same play (no foul and warning on the same play). Foul = No warning. No foul = Warning.

a 停止比赛计时钟手势。

b 做出"前臂上抬两次"手势。

c 做出"技术犯规"手势。

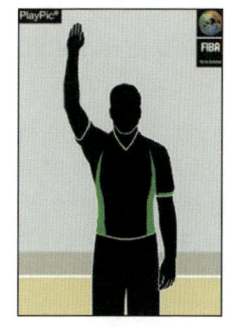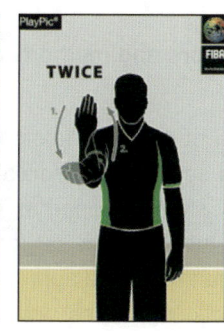

骗取犯规的一些迹象：

- 骗取犯规者抢先找接触（他需要靠一次接触来制造骗取犯规）。
- 在并没有发生头部接触时头部向后移动（头部骗取犯规）。
- 做出戏剧性的、夸张的动作。
- 起跳点和落地点相互间距离很近。
- 倒地时高高抬起脚，双手做好了倒地准备。

以下并不总是骗取犯规情况：

- 当一名运球队员为创造空间而延展手臂时——原则上这依然是一起进攻犯规。
- 当一名队员因踩到另一名队员而失去平衡——原则上这不是一次骗取犯规。

完整看清比赛情况至关重要，这不单指看队员的反应。非法接触依然会被宣判为犯规，附带接触依然是比赛的一部分且合法。如果在比赛情况中发生了一次犯规，那么同一个比赛情况中就不可能发生骗取犯规（反之则是无犯规并警告）。犯规 = 无警告，无犯规 = 警告。

2.14 CONTROL OF THE GAME AND SHOT CLOCK

Target:
- **Identify the correct techniques of how to control the game & shot clock.**
- **Identify the most common play situation where a possible error might occur.**
- **Identify the correct procedure and methods of how to re-set the game or shot clock.**

The control of the game & shot clock by referees has become a standard routine nowadays. Five years ago it was practically inexistent or at the least very rare. It has been previously questioned as to how a referee is able to control the clocks almost all the time and still focus fully on play situations. The secret is in the correct technique and appropriate timing. This combined with thousands of repetitive actions(practise) will ensure it becomes automatic skill (developed and maintained in your muscle memory). The basic element being that game clock will be controlled every time there is new team control.

Note: These techniques work when timing displays are visible to the referees.

Phase 1	Learn to control game clock
Game clock -when it should be started	**Starting the game clock when:** A. During a jump ball, the ball is legally tapped by a jumper. B. After an unsuccessful last or only free throw and the ball continues to be live, the ball touches or is touched by a player on the playing court. C. During a throw-in, the ball touches or is legally touched by a player on the playing court.
Game clock -when it should be stopped	**Stopping the game clock when:** A. Time expires at the end of playing time for a quarter, if not stopped automatically by the game clock itself. B. A referee blows his whistle while the ball is live. C. A field goal is scored against a team which has requested a time-out. D. A field goal is scored when the game clock shows 2:00 minutes or less in the fourth quarter and in each overtime. E. The shot clock signal sounds while a team is in control of the ball.

2.14 比赛和进攻计时钟的掌控

目标：
- 确认正确掌控比赛和进攻计时钟的技术。
- 确认可能发生错误的最常见的情况。
- 确认重新比赛以及复位进攻计时的正确步骤和方法。

裁判员对比赛和进攻计时钟的掌控，如今已经变成了常规的标准，五年前这在实践中是不存在的或是很稀有的。一名裁判员在比赛全程可以掌控时间的同时又全身心专注于比赛场上的情况，这之前就被质疑过。秘诀就在于正确的技术和恰当的计时。这种结合了上千次的重复动作将会保证它成为自动化的技术（形成和保持于你的肌肉记忆）。每当出现新的球权时，比赛计时钟就会被控制。

注意：当裁判员可以看见计时钟时这些技术就要使用。

阶段 1	学习如何掌控比赛计时钟
什么时候比赛计时开始	**在下列情况下应开启比赛计时钟** A. 跳球时，球被跳球队员合法拍击。 B. 当最后一次或仅有的一次罚球失败，球仍是活球，球接触到或被场上一名队员接触。 C. 掷球入界时，球触碰场上的队员或被场上的队员合法触碰。
什么时候比赛计时停止	**下列情况下应停止比赛计时钟** A. 当一节的时间结束，如果比赛时间没有自动停止。 B. 活球情况下，裁判员鸣哨。 C. 中篮得分时对方队伍请求暂停。 D. 四节或决胜期比赛计时钟显示还有 2 分钟或更少时，有球队得分。 E. 当一个队控制球时，进攻计时信号响起。

Phase 2	Learn to control game clock whenever there is a new team possession

Team establishes a new team control possession (new shot clock period)

Pick up the game clock:
A. Pick up the last two digits of the game clock.
B. Example: 6:26 -> pick up the 26.
C. Whenever you have to correct the shot clock, you know the game clock time and when the shot clock period started.
D. Example: 6:26 - new team possession -> ball goes out of bounds and shot clock is re-set by mistake. When the game clock shows 6:10, the Referee can determine the shot clock with some basic mathematics: 26–10=16(therefore 16 seconds has elapsed). The new correct shotclock time is 8 seconds.

Most common situations when errors occur with timing

A. Jump ball - legally tap (start game clock) and first possession (shot clock).
B. Out of bound play (stop game clock).
C. Throw-in (start game clock).
D. Rebound play - new possession (shot clock).
E. Saving ball from out of bounds play (if new control or not – shot clock).
F. "Loose ball" but not a change of team control (re-set clock by mistake).

Phase 3	Learn to control game and shot clock in the end of quarter

New team control and 24.0 / 14.0 seconds or less on the game clock

When you have 24.0/14.0* seconds or less on the game and there is a new team control

1. One of the referees indicates this by showing one finger.
2. The other referee(s) will copy the signal (mirroring).
3. This means: it is possible that the quarter will end during this team's control.
4. All referees should get ready to pay close attention to the game clock in order to determine in a last moment shot situation whether the shot has been taken in time – A valid basket or not (cancelled basket).

* in case of offensive rebound or throw-in from front court according to OBR article 29.2.1

阶段 2	每当有新球队拥有球权时学会掌控比赛计时钟
一个球队建立新的球权控制（新进攻计时周期）监控比赛计时钟	选取比赛计时钟 A. 选取比赛计时钟的最后两位数。 B. 比如 6:26 选取 26。 C. 每当你要校准进攻计时钟时，要知道比赛计时钟的时间和什么时候进攻计时开始。 D. 比如，在 6:26 时球出界，新球权拥有队，进攻计时因为失误而复位。当比赛时间显示 6:10 时，裁判可以依靠基本的数学计算决定进攻计时，26–10=16（因此就走过了 16 秒）。新进攻计时就是 8 秒。 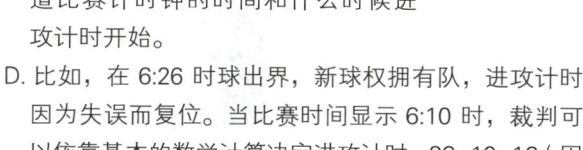
计时错误发生的最普通的情况 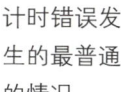	A. 跳球——合法拍击（比赛计时开始），球权建立（进攻计时开始）。 B. 球出界（比赛计时停止）。 C. 掷球入界（比赛计时开始）。 D. 篮板球——球权转换（进攻计时开始）。 E. 从界外救球（是否球权转换——进攻计时）。 F. 掉球，但没有转换球权（比赛计时钟误回）。

阶段 3	学习在每节临近结束的时候掌控比赛和进攻计时钟
新的球队建立球权而比赛只剩 24.0/14.0 秒或更少	当球权转换后比赛只剩 24.0/14.0 * 秒或更少 1. 一名裁判员通过一个手指来表示这一点。 2. 其他裁判员重复手势（予以回应）。 3. 这意味着在这个球队的控制下比赛有可能结束。 4. 所有裁判员应准备密切关注比赛时钟，以确定在最后一刻的投篮是否在有效时间内完成——有效的投篮或者不是有效的投篮（进球无效）。 * 根据《篮球规则》中 29.2.1 所述的进攻篮板球和前场掷球入界情况。 

 **FIBA REFEREES MANUAL**

Phase 3	Learn to control game and shot clock in the end of quarter

Procedure when signal sounds / LED lights appear for the end of the quarter.

1. Referee blows the whistle immediately and raises his hand.

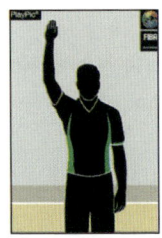

2. If the basket is valid (ball is released before the signal sounds / LED lights appear), the referee keeps the hand up and when ball goes into the basket shows the basket count signal (2/3 points).

3. If the basket is to be cancelled (ball is still in the hand of the shooter when the signal sounds / LED lights appear), the referee indicates immediately the "cancel basket" signal.

 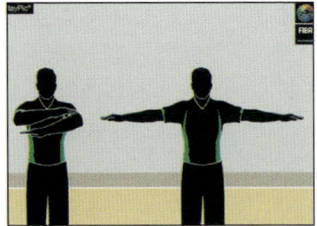

国际篮联裁判员手册

| 阶段 3 | 学习在每节临近结束的时候掌控比赛和进攻计时钟 |

当一节比赛结束的信号声音响起/LED 灯亮起时要执行的程序

1. 裁判员立即鸣哨，举起手来。

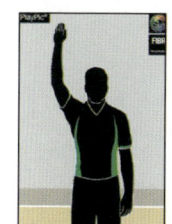

2. 如果投篮是有效的（球在信号响起/LED 灯亮之前出手），裁判员保持手向上，当球进入球篮后做出得分有效手势（2/3 分）。

3. 如果进球无效（当信号声响起/LED 灯亮时，球仍在投篮队员手中），裁判员立即做出"进球无效"手势。

 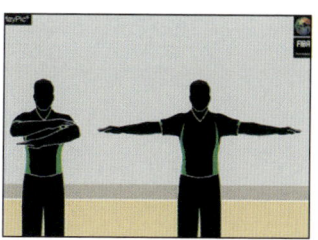

49

第 3 章
SIGNALS & TERMINOLOGY
手势和术语

 FIBA REFEREES MANUAL

CHAPTER 3

3. SIGNALS & TERMINOLOGY

3.1 OFFICIAL REFEREES' SIGNALS

Game clock signals

STOP THE CLOCK
Open palm

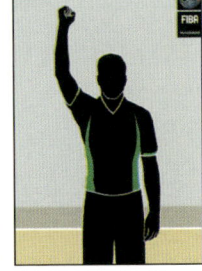
STOP THE CLOCK FOR FOUL
One clenched fist

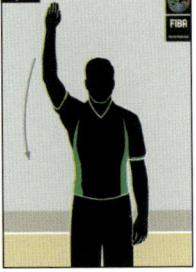
START THE CLOCK
Chop with hand

Scoring

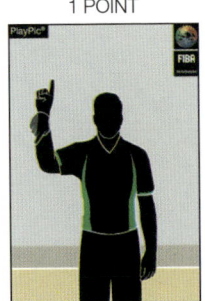
1 POINT
1 finger, 'flag' from wrist

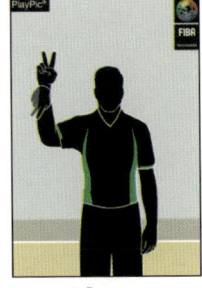
2 POINTS
2 fingers, 'flag' from wrist

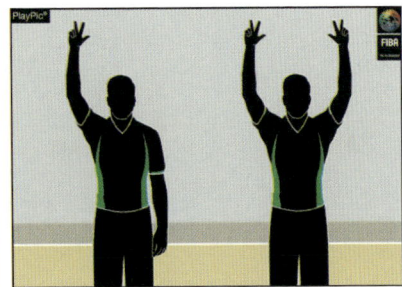
3 POINTS
3 fingers extended
One arm: Attempt
Both arms: Successful

第 3 章

3. 手势和术语

3.1 官方裁判员手势

比赛计时钟信号

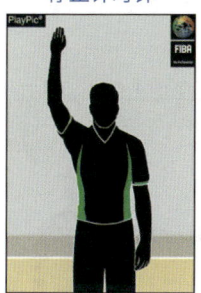

停止计时钟
伸开手掌

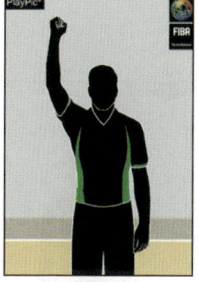

犯规停止计时钟
一拳紧握

计时开始
用手做砍劈

得分

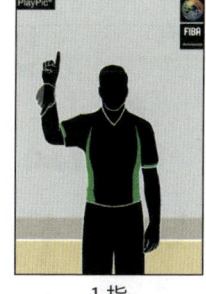

1 分
1 指
从腕部下屈

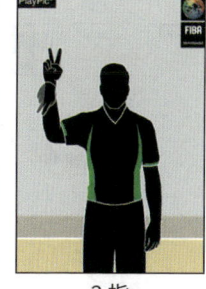

2 分
2 指
从腕部下屈

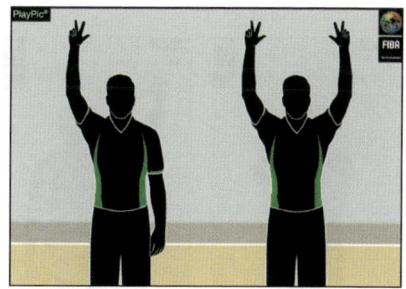

3 分
伸展 3 指
一只胳膊：3 分试投
两只胳膊：3 分投篮成功

 FIBA REFEREES MANUAL

Substitution and Time-out

SUBSTITUTION
Cross forearms

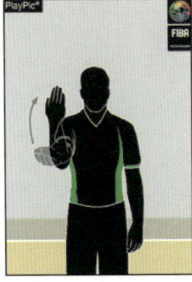
BECKONING-IN
Open palm, wave towards the body

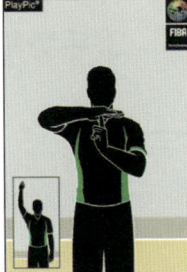
CHARGED TIME-OUT
Form T, show index finger

MEDIA TIME-OUT
Open arms with clenched fists

Informative

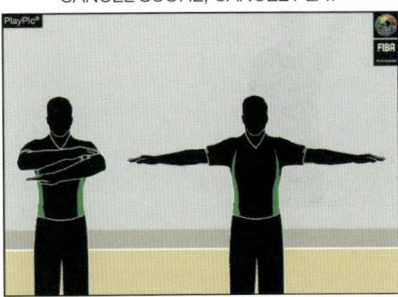
CANCEL SCORE, CANCEL PLAY
Scissor-like action with arms, once across chest

VISIBLE COUNT
Counting while moving the palm

COMMUNICATION
Thumb up

SHOT CLOCK RESET
Rotate hand, extend index finger

DIRECTION OF PLAY AND/OR OUT-OF-BOUNDS
Point in direction of play, arm parallel to sidelines

HELD BALL/JUMP BALL SITUATION
Thumbs up, then point in direction of play using the alternating possession arrow

替换和暂停

替换	招呼入场	暂停	媒体暂停
	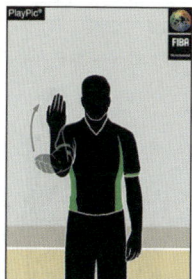		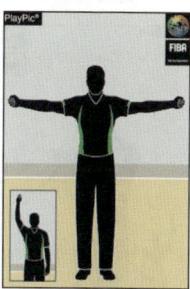
前臂交叉	伸出手掌摆向身体	成"T"形食指示之	张开双臂紧握拳头

提供信息

取消得分，中止比赛	可见的计数
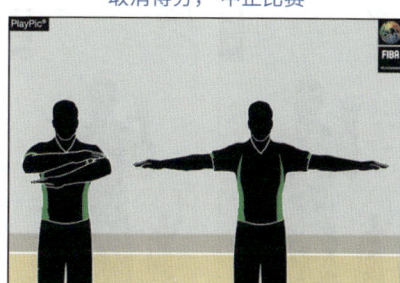	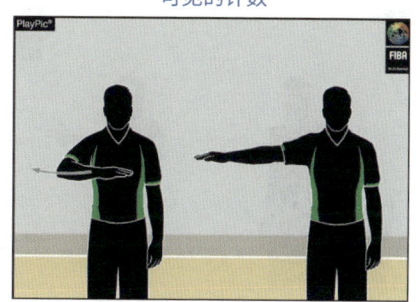
双臂像剪的动作，胸前交叉一次	移动手掌计数

交流	进攻计时钟复位	比赛方向和/或出界	争球/跳球情况
	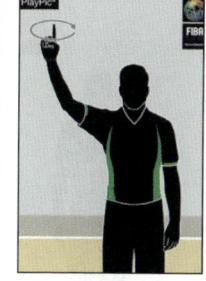		
拇指向上	伸出食指并转动手	指向比赛方向，手臂与边线平行	两拇指向上，然后指向交替拥有箭头所指的比赛方向

 FIBA REFEREES MANUAL

Violations

TRAVELLING	ILLEGAL DRIBBLE: DOUBLE DRIBBLING	ILLEGAL DRIBBLE: CARRYING THE BALL

  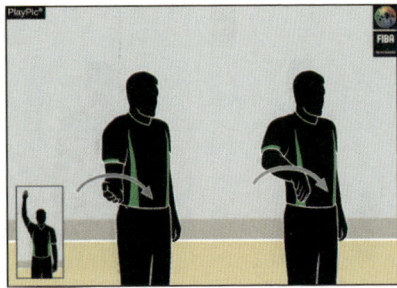

Rotate fists	Patting motion with palm	Half rotation with palm

3 SECONDS	5 SECONDS	8 SECONDS

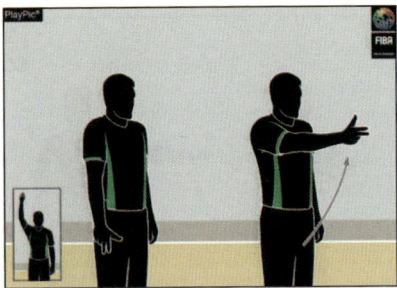  

Arm extended, show 3 fingers	Show 5 fingers	Show 8 fingers

24 SECONDS	BALL RETURNED TO BACKCOURT	DELIBERATE KICK OR BLOCK OF THE BALL

 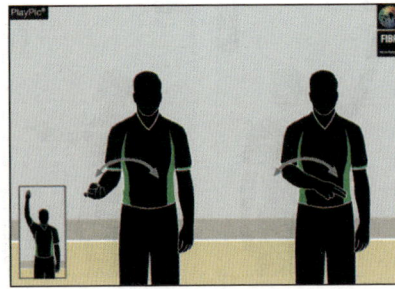 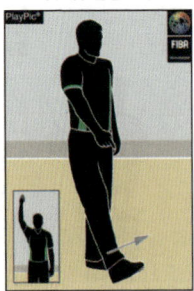

Fingers touch shoulder	Wave arm front of body	Point to the foot

违例

带球走
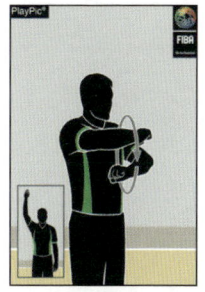
转动双拳

非法运球:两次运球
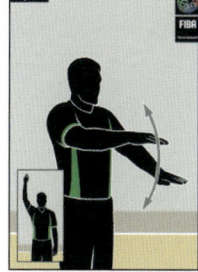
用手掌做轻拍动作

非法运球:携带球
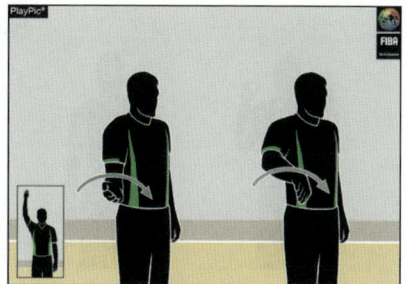
半转手掌

3 秒钟
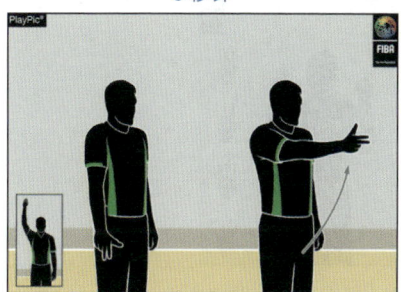
伸出手臂示 3 指

5 秒钟

示 5 指

8 秒钟

示 8 指

24 秒钟
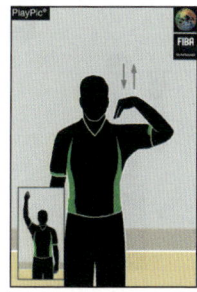
手指触肩

球回后场
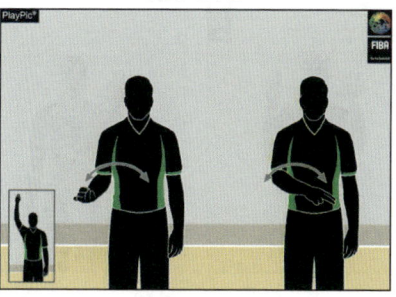
身前摆动手臂

故意脚踢或拦阻球
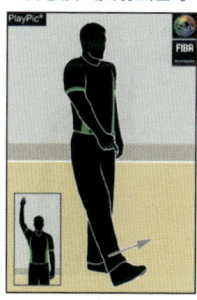
手指指脚

Number of Players

No. 00 and 0

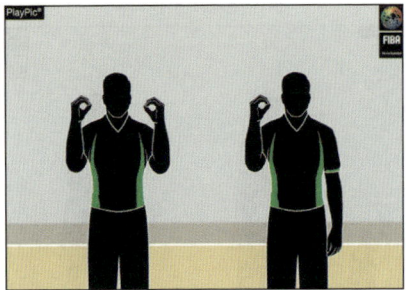

Both hands show number 0

Right hand shows number 0

No. 1 - 5

Right hand shows number 1 to 5

No. 6 - 10

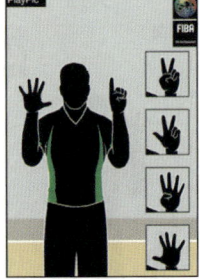

Right hand shows number 5, left hand shows number 1 to 5

No. 11 - 15

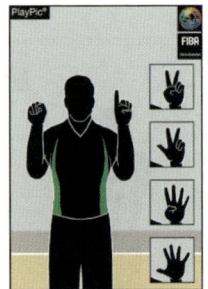

Right hand shows clenched fist, left hand shows number 1 to 5

No. 16

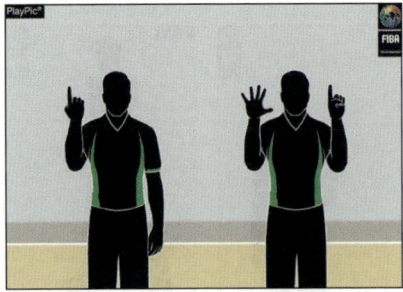

First reverse hand shows number 1 for the decade digit - then open hands show number 6 for the units digit

No. 24

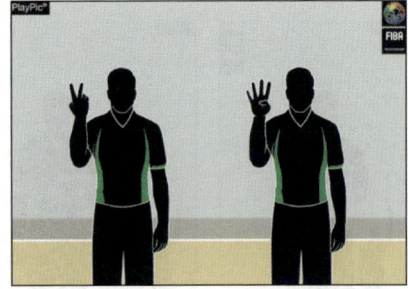

First reverse hand shows number 2 for the decade digit - then open hand shows number 4 for the units digit

队员的号码

No.00 和 No.0

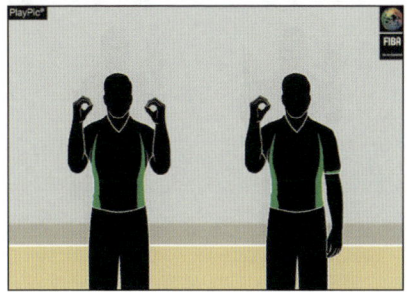

双手示 0 号　　　右手示 0 号

No.1-5

右手示号码 1 到 5

No.6-10

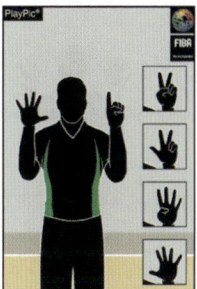

右手示 5 号，
左手示号码 1 到 5

No.11-15

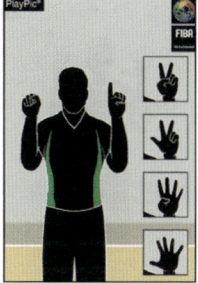

右手示紧握的拳头，
左手示号码 1 到 5

No.16

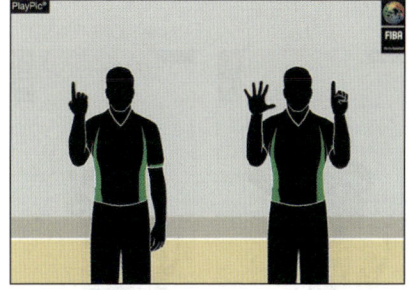

首先手背朝外示 1 号代表十位数，
然后手掌朝外示 6 号代表个位数

No.24

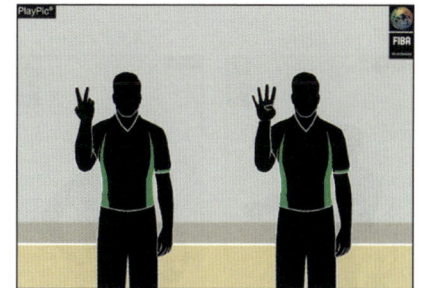

首先手背朝外示 2 号代表十位数，
然后手掌朝外示 4 号代表个位数

No. 40

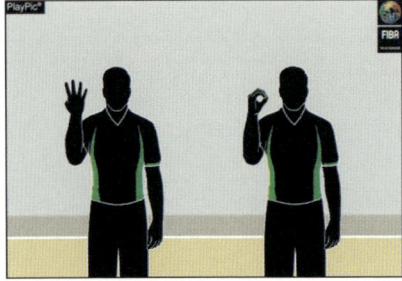

First reverse hand shows number 4 for the decade digit - then open hand shows number 0 for the units digit

No. 62

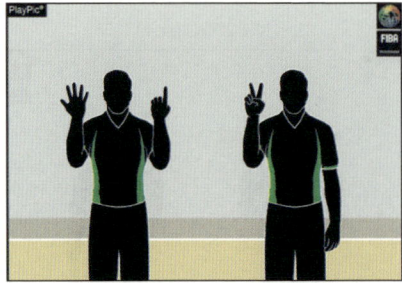

First reverse hands show number 6 for the decade digit - then open hand shows number 2 for the units digit

No. 78

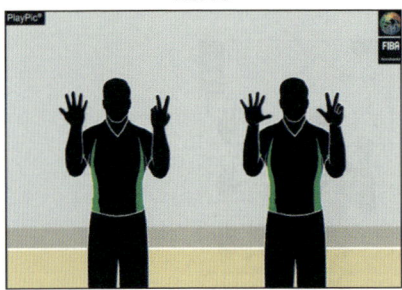

First reverse hands show number 7 for the decade digit - then open hands show number 8 for the units digit

No. 99

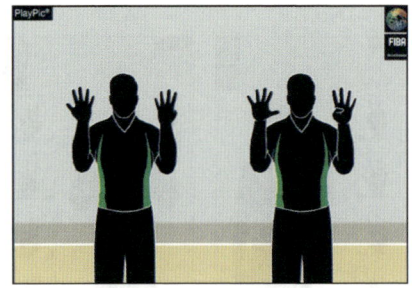

First reverse hands show number 9 for the decade digit - then open hands show number 9 for the units digit

Type of Fouls

HOLDING	BLOCKING (DEFENSE), ILLEGAL SCREEN (OFFENSE)	PUSHING OR CHARGING WITHOUT THE BALL	HANDCHECKING
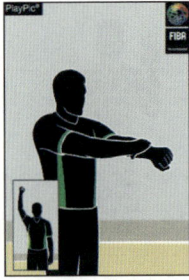			
Grasp wrist downward	Both hands on hips	Imitate push	Grab palm and forward motion

No.40
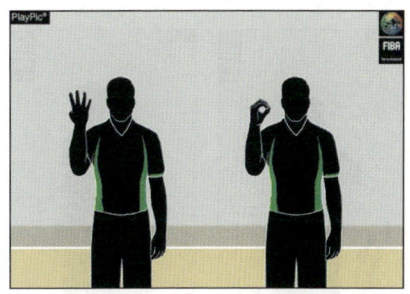
首先手背朝外示 4 号代表十位数，
然后手掌朝外示 0 号代表个位数

No.62
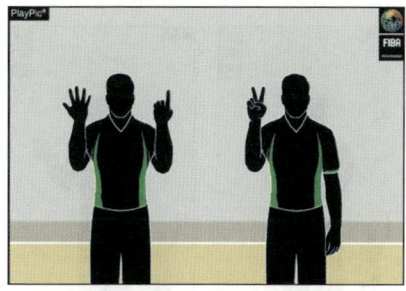
首先手背朝外示 6 号代表十位数，
然后手掌朝外示 2 号代表个位数

No.78
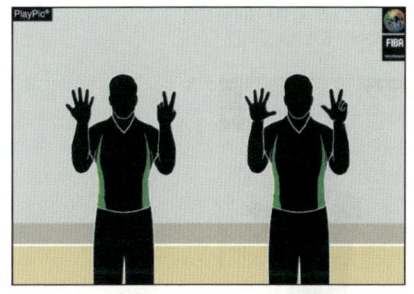
首先手背朝外示 7 号代表十位数，
然后手掌朝外示 8 号代表个位数

No.99
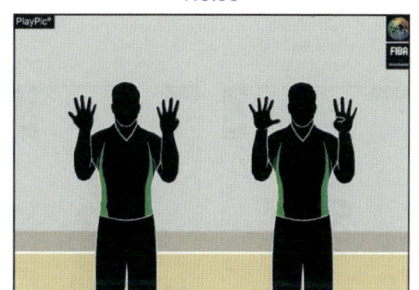
首先手背朝外示 9 号代表十位数，
然后手掌朝外示 9 号代表个位数

犯规的类型

拉人

阻挡（防守）
非法掩护（进攻）

推人或
不带球撞人

用手推挡

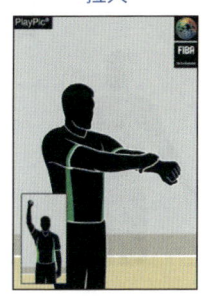

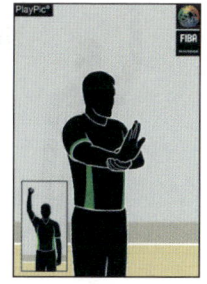

向下抓住手腕　　双手置髋部　　模仿推　　抓住手掌向前移动

FIBA REFEREES MANUAL

ILLEGAL USE OF HANDS

Strike wrist

CHARGING WITH THE BALL

Clenched fist strike open palm

ILLEGAL CONTACT TO THE HAND

Strike the palm towards the other forearm

HOOKING
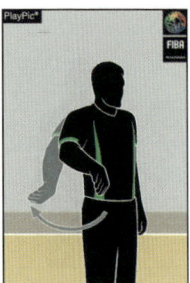
Move lower arm backwards

EXCESSIVE SWINGING OF ELBOW

Swing elbow backwards

HIT TO THE HEAD

Imitate the contact to the head

FOUL BY TEAM IN CONTROL OF THE BALL

Point clenched fist towards basket of offending team

FOUL ON THE ACT OF SHOOTING
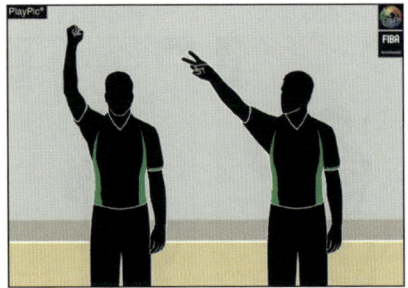
One arm with clenched fist, followed by indication of the number of free throws

FOUL NOT ON THE ACT OF SHOOTING
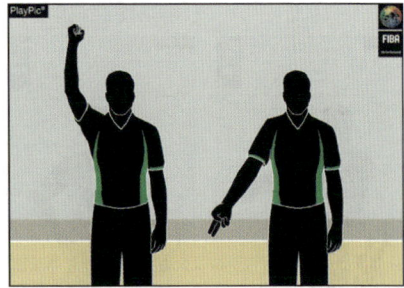
One arm with clenched fist, followed by pointing to the floor

非法用手	带球撞人	对手的非法接触	勾人犯规
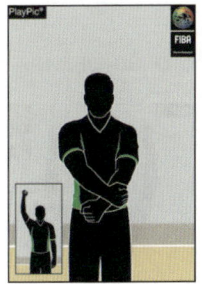			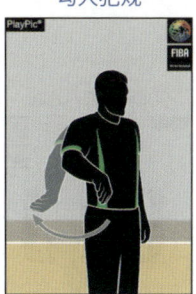
击腕	握拳击掌	掌击另一只前臂	向后移动前臂

过分挥肘	击头	控制球队的犯规
		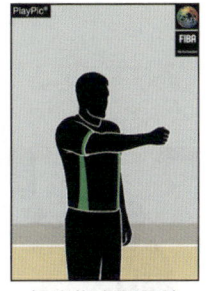
向后摆肘	模仿拍击头部	握拳指向犯规队的球篮

对投篮动作的犯规	对非投篮动作的犯规
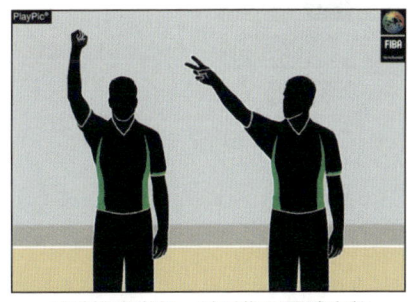	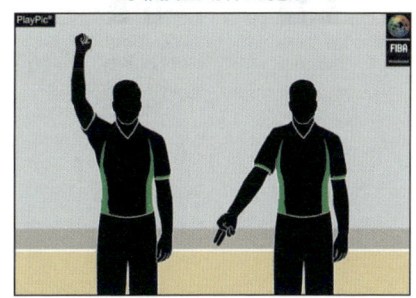
单臂握拳举起，随后指示罚球次数	单臂握拳举起，随后指向地面

Special Fouls

DOUBLE FOUL	TECHNICAL FOUL	UNSPORTS-MANLIKE FOUL	DISQUALIFYING FOUL
	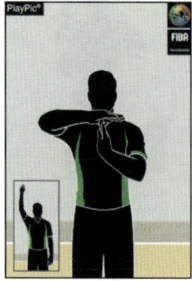		
Wave clenched fists on both hands	Form T, showing palms	Grasp wrist upward	Clenched fists on both hands

FAKE A FOUL	ILLEGAL BOUNDARY LINE CROSSING ON A THROW-IN	IRS REVIEW
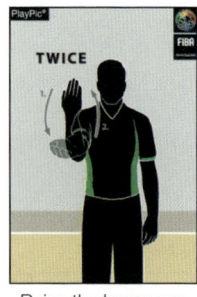		
Raise the lower arm twice	Wave arm parallel to boundary line (in last 2 minutes of the fourth quarter and overtime)	Rotate hand with horizontal extended index finger

特殊犯规

双方犯规

挥动紧握的双拳

技术犯规

成"T"形手掌示之

违反体育运动精神的犯规

向上抓住手腕

取消比赛资格的犯规

紧握双拳

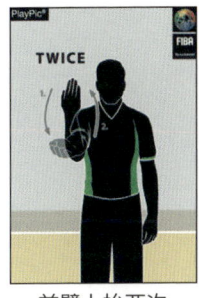

骗取犯规

前臂上抬两次
(从高处做起)

掷球入界非法越线

平行于界线摆动手臂(第4节和决胜期最后2:00分钟)

调用即时回放系统

水平伸直食指转动手

FIBA REFEREES MANUAL

Foul Penalty Administration – Reporting to Table

AFTER FOUL WITHOUT FREE THROW(S)

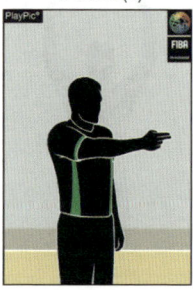

Point in direction of play, arm parallel to sidelines

AFTER FOUL BY TEAM IN CONTROL OF THE BALL

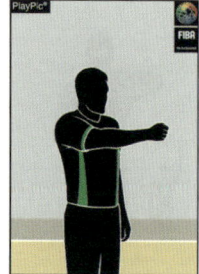

Clenched fist in direction of play, arm parallel to sidelines

1 FREE THROW

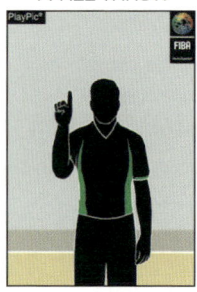

Hold up 1 finger

2 FREE THROWS

Hold up 2 fingers

3 FREE THROWS

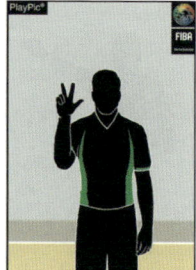

Hold up 3 fingers

向记录台报告罚则

没有罚球的犯规后

指向比赛方向，
手臂与边线平行

控制球队犯规后

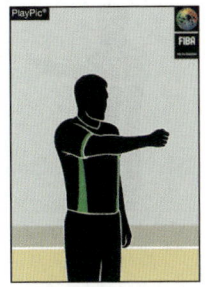

握拳指向比赛方向
手臂与边线平行

1 次罚球

举起 1 指

2 次罚球

举起 2 指

3 次罚球

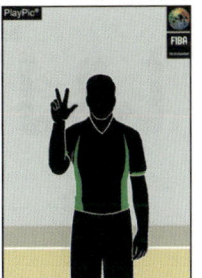

举起 3 指

Administrating Free Throws – Active Referee (Lead)

1 FREE THROW

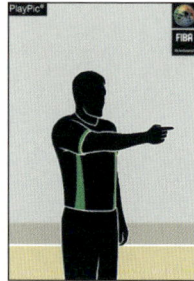

1 finger horizontal

2 FREE THROWS

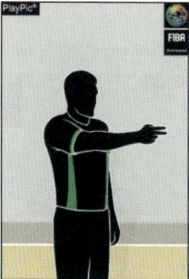

2 fingers horizontal

3 FREE THROWS

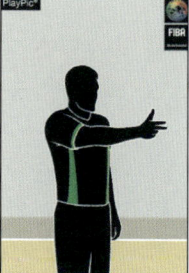

3 fingers horizontal

Administrating Free Throws – Passive Referee (Trail in 2PO & Centre in 3PO)

1 FREE THROW

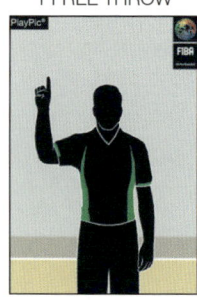

Index finger

2 FREE THROWS

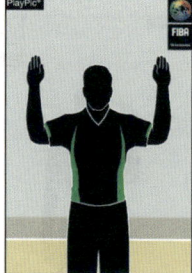

Fingers together on both hands

3 FREE THROWS

3 fingers extended on both hands

罚球管理——执行裁判（前导裁判）

1 次罚球

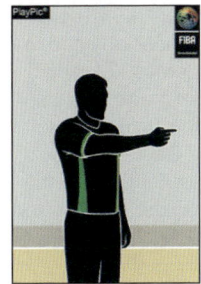

水平伸 1 指

2 次罚球

水平伸 2 指

3 次罚球

水平伸 3 指

罚球管理——非执行裁判（2 人执裁之追踪裁判与 3 人执裁之中央裁判）

1 次罚球

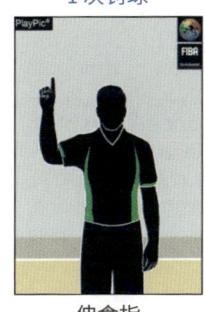

伸食指

2 次罚球

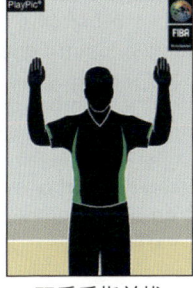

双手手指并拢

3 次罚球

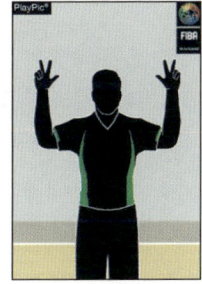

双手伸展 3 指

3.2 BASIC BASKETBALL OFFICIATING TERMINOLOGY

TERM	ABBR	EXPLANATION
45° (Forty five degrees)	45°	This refers to the preferred angle of the referees' stance, especially in Lead and Trail positions and in some cases by Centre as well. Referees in L and T position will normally face the basket and maintain a 45° angle in order to keep in the field of vision as many players as possible. The Centre referee's basic stance is generally flat with his/her back to the sideline, but Centre will normally adjust position to approximately 45° during weak side drives.
Act of Shooting	AOS	The act of shooting on a shot: • Begins when the player starts, in the judgement of a referee, to move the ball upwards towards the opponents' basket. • Ends when the ball has left the player's hand(s), or if an entirely new act of shooting is made and, in case of an airborne shooter, both feet have returned to the floor. The act of shooting in a continuous movement on drives to the basket or other moving shots: • Begins when the ball has come to rest in the player's hand(s), upon completion of a dribble or a catch in the air and the player starts, in the judgment of the referee, the shooting motion preceding the release of the ball for a field goal. • Ends when the ball has left the player's hand(s), or if an entirely new act of shooting is made and, in case of an airborne shooter, both feet have returned to the floor.
Action Area	AA	Action Area may involve players with or without the ball. Knowledge on various play situations (pick & roll, screening, post-ups, rebounding) will help referees identify Action Areas in their primary, or when extending or expanding coverage.
Active Mindset	AMI	Refereeing is nothing but being ready. Good referees are constantly analysing the movements and actions of the players in order to be in position to see something illegal. Look for reasons to call (illegal).

3.2 篮球裁判基本术语

（译者注：下列术语缩写中的 N/A 表示"不适用"，即无缩写形式）

术语	缩写	解释
45度 （四十五度）	45°	这是指裁判员站立落位的首选角度，特别是前导裁判和追踪裁判的视角，以及在某些情况下的中央裁判。裁判在 L 和 T 的位置通常会面向球，并保持 45° 的角度，以保障尽可能多的队员在他的视野中。中央裁判的基本姿势是背对边线，但他通常会在弱侧有情况时以大概 45° 的角度适当调整位置。
投篮动作	AOS	投篮动作： • 开始于：根据裁判员的判断，当队员将球朝着对方球篮做向上的动作时。 • 结束于：球已离开队员的手，或者做了一个全新的投篮动作时。如果是跳起在空中的投篮队员，他必须双脚落回地面。 突破上篮或其他运动中投篮的连续动作： • 开始于：根据裁判员的判断，当队员结束运球或在空中接到球后，球已在手中停留时，队员在球离手前开始做投篮的连续动作。 • 结束于：球已离开队员的手，或者做了一个全新的投篮动作时。如果是跳起在空中的投篮队员，他必须双脚落回地面。
动态区	AA	动态区域可能涉及有球和无球队员。了解各种球场上的情况（挡拆、掩护、策应、篮板），这将有助于裁判员辨认主要行动区域，或扩大视野覆盖范围。
动态思维	AMI	执裁就是时刻准备。优秀的裁判员会不断分析队员的动作和行为，并始终追求最佳站位以观察非法动作，寻求判罚的理由（非法）。

TERM	ABBR	EXPLANATION
Active Referee	AR	The referee who hands the ball to a free throw shooter or player for a throw-in, or to administer the jump ball to start the game.
Alternating Possession	AP	Alternating possession is a method of causing the ball to become live with a throw-in rather than a jump ball.
Alternating Possession Arrow	APA	The team entitled to the alternating possession throw-in shall be indicated by the alternating possession arrow in the direction of the opponents' basket. The direction of the alternating possession arrow will be reversed immediately when the alternating possession throw in ends.
Angle(s)	N/A	Working the angles; that is attempting to maintain a line of vision where the referee can see between players in order to keep vision on the areas of greatest potential contact.
Anticipate (call)	AC	Describes the situation when a referee anticipates that a certain event will occur and blows the whistle before actually seeing and reflecting on the event. Usually, this refers to the case when the referee makes a mistake because what they anticipated did not, in actuality, occur.
Anticipate (play)	APL	Describes the situation when a referee is able to read the play and anticipate the next moves to come and is able to adjust position/angle properly in advance of covering the upcoming play.
Assistant Scorer	ASC	The assistant scorer shall operate the scoreboard and assist the scorer. In the case of any discrepancy between the scoreboard and the scoresheet which cannot be resolved, the scoresheet shall take precedence and the scoreboard shall be corrected accordingly.
At the Disposal (Ball)	BATD	When a referee hands the ball to a player making a throw-in or shooting a free throw or the referee is placing the ball at the disposal of the player.
Authorised Signals	N/A	Authorised Signals: Those signals made by the referee for official communication to players or the bench as outlined by the FIBA Basketball Rules.

术语	缩写	解释
执行裁判	AR	指把球给执行罚球或掷球入界的队员，或者开场执行跳球的裁判员。
交替拥有	AP	交替拥有是以掷球入界而不是以跳球使球成活球的一种方法。
交替拥有箭头	APA	交替拥有箭头应当指向拥有球权的球队的进攻方向。当交替拥有球权的掷球入界结束，箭头的方向应当立即翻转。
角度	N/A	选择合适的角度，是试图保持好的视线，裁判可以看到队员之间的行为，以保证视野里能看到更多的区域和潜在的一些接触。
预先（宣判）	AC	这是指当裁判员预判会发生某些事件并在确实看到之前响哨的情况。通常，这是裁判员犯错误的情况，因为他们所预期的事件并不是实际发生的。
预见（比赛）	APL	这是指当裁判员能够阅读比赛并判断队员下一步的动作，可以在覆盖即将到来的比赛之前适当调整自己在球场的位置/角度。
助理记录员	ASC	助理记录员应操作记录大屏并协助记录员。当记录大屏与记录表之间存在差异无法解决的情况下，应该根据记录表优先更正记录大屏。
可处理（球）	BATD	裁判员将球交给一个执行掷球入界或准备罚球的队员，或者裁判员将球放在队员的处理球的位置上。
正规手势	N/A	正规手势：如国际篮联官方篮球规则的解释，这些手势是裁判员与队员或球队席的交流的信号。

TERM	ABBR	EXPLANATION
Backboard	BB	The wood or glass rectangle on which the ring is suspended. The official size is 1.8m wide and 1.05m high. The ring is centred on the "board" 15cm from the base on the board.
Backcourt	BC	A team's backcourt consists of its team's own basket, the inbounds part of the backboard and that part of the playing court limited by the endline behind their own basket, the sidelines and the centre line.
Backcourt Violation	BCV	Where an offensive player with the ball in their frontcourt causes the ball to go into the backcourt where it is first touched by them or a teammate. Also called an "over and back" violation.
Ball Side	BS	This refers to the position of the ball. When the playing court is divided by an imaginary line extending from basket to basket, the side of the playing court on which the ball is located is called the "ball-side".
Basket Interference	BI	Basket interference occurs when: • After a shot for a field goal or the last or only free throw a player touches the basket or the backboard while the ball is in contact with the ring. • After a free throw followed by an additional free throw(s), a player touches the ball, the basket or the backboard while there is still a possibility that the ball will enter the basket. • A player reaches through the basket from below and touches the ball. • A defensive player touches the ball or the basket while the ball is within the basket, thus preventing the ball from passing through the basket. • A player causes the basket to vibrate or grasps the basket in such a way that, in the judgement of a referee, the ball has been prevented from entering the basket or has been caused to enter the basket. • A player grasps the basket to play the ball.

术语	缩写	解释
篮板	BB	这个篮板是指木头或玻璃矩形上并且挂着球篮。官方篮板尺寸长 1.8 米，宽 1.05 米。球篮为"篮板"的中心，篮圈和篮板下沿之间有 15 厘米的距离。
后场	BC	一个球队的后场是由本方球篮、篮板的界内部分，以及由该队本方球篮后面的端线、两条边线和中线所界定的比赛场地部分组成。
球回后场违例	BCV	在前场控制活球的进攻队员使球回到后场并首先被同队队员触及，又叫做"回场违例"。
球侧	BS	这是指球的位置。当比赛场地由一个球篮到球篮之间的假想线从中间分开，球所在的一侧称为"球侧"。
干扰得分	BI	干扰得分发生于： • 在一次投篮或最后一次罚球中，当球与球篮接触时，队员触及球篮或篮板。 • 在一次罚球（随后还有进一步的罚球）后，球有进入球篮的可能性时，一名队员触及球、球篮或篮板时。 • 队员从下方伸手穿过球篮并触及球时。 • 当球在球篮中，防守队员触及球或球篮，从而阻止球通过球篮时。 • 队员使篮板颤动或者抓球篮，根据裁判员的判定，这种手段已妨碍球进入球篮或者使球进入球篮时。 • 队员抓球篮打球时。

TERM	ABBR	EXPLANATION
Bench Control	N/A	Referees ensuring that the players and coaches sitting on the bench do not violate the rules of sportsmanship.
Blocking	BL	Blocking is illegal personal contact which impedes the progress of an opponent with or without the ball.
Bonus	N/A	When two free throws are granted to a player when he/she has been fouled and their opponent's team has reached the limit of four team fouls in a quarter.
Boundary Lines	N/A	The playing court shall be limited by the boundary lines, consisting of the endlines and the sidelines. These lines are not part of the playing court.
Buzzer	N/A	Signal from the scorer's table used to indicate substitutions, time outs, disqualifications and end of quarters, or may be used by table officials to summon a referee to confer in the case of a misunderstood ruling.
Cancel the Score (basket)	N/A	A referee signals that a basket which has been made is to be discounted i.e. when a player charges when shooting with contact occurring before the ball leaves the shooters hands – the referee cancels the score indicating to the scorer's table that the basket does not count.
Captain	CAP	The captain (CAP) is a player designated by team's head coach to represent the team on the playing court. The captain may communicate in a courteous manner with the referees during the game to obtain information, however, only when the ball becomes dead and the game clock is stopped.
Centre (Referee)	C	The Centre referee (3PO) is the official who is positioned on the opposite side of the frontcourt from the Lead (usually opposite side of the ball) at the free-throw line extended (set-up position). Depending on the location of the ball, Centre may be on either side of the frontcourt.

术语	缩写	解释
球队席控制	N/A	裁判员确保坐在球队席上的队员和教练不违反体育运动精神规则。
阻挡	BL	阻挡是非法的身体接触，阻碍有球或无球的对手行进。
追加（罚球）	N/A	当一名队员被犯规，并且对方球队犯规次数已经累计达到了四次时，该队员获得两次罚球。
边界线	N/A	球场由界线包括端线和边线限定。这些线不是比赛场地的一部分。
蜂鸣器	N/A	记录台用来指示替换、暂停、取消比赛资格，或是在每一节末，或可用于记录台人员出现疑问后需要引起裁判员注意时所使用的发出信号的工具。
取消得分	N/A	裁判员做出中篮不计得分的手势，例：当一名队员在投篮出手前发生撞人犯规后，裁判取消得分并向记录台示意中篮无效。
队长	CAP	队长（CAP）是一名由主教练指定的在比赛场地上代表他的球队的队员。在比赛期间，队长可与裁判员联系以获得信息，但是做此举要有礼貌，而且只能在球成死球和比赛计时钟停止时进行。
中央裁判	C	中央裁判（3人执裁）是位于前场的在前导裁判对面（通常在球侧对面）且在罚球线延长线位置的裁判员（初始位置）。取决于球的位置，中央裁判可能出现在前场的任意一侧。

77

TERM	ABBR	EXPLANATION
Centre Line	N/A	The line designating the halfway mark of the court.
Charge (Charging)	CH	Charging is illegal personal contact, with or without the ball, by pushing or moving into an opponent's torso.
Close Down	CD	The position of the Lead where he should move before actual rotation starts.
Closed Angle	CA	A stacked or straight-lined view of the action area in a referee's primary / secondary coverage area.
Commissioner	COM	The commissioner shall sit between the scorer and the timer. Commissioners primary duty during the game is to supervise the work of the table officials and to assist the crew chief and umpire(s) in the smooth functioning of the game.
Consistency	N/A	A referee who interprets play situations and criteria exactly the same way throughout is said to be consistent.
Contact Foul	N/A	A personal foul resulting from a player illegally touching another player and putting him at a disadvantage.
Control of the Ball	COB	A team is said to be in control of the ball when a player of that team first has the ball in their possession inbounds or when the ball is placed at their disposal for a throw-in. It extends until the time a shot is taken, a whistle blows, or a player from the opposition side gains control. A player is in control of the ball when they are holding a live ball in their hands or dribbling it, or when the ball is at their disposal for a throw-in or a free throw.
Correctable Errors	CE	Referees may correct an error if a rule is inadvertently disregarded in the following situations only: • Awarding an unmerited free throw(s). • Failure to award a merited free throw(s). • Erroneous awarding or cancelling of a point(s). • Permitting the wrong player to attempt a free throw(s).
Coverage	CG	The vision on the game of the two/three referees; good coverage means that the referees between them have all players in sight both on and off the ball.

术语	缩写	解释
中线	N/A	指明全场中心标志的线。
撞人	GH	撞人是非法的侵入身体接触，有球或无球，推或移动对手的躯干。
轮转发起点	CD	轮转启动之前，前导裁判员需提前抵达的位置。
闭角	CA	在一名裁判员的主/次要责任区内出现的被遮挡的或是三点一线的视角。
技术代表	COM	技术代表应坐在记录员和计时员之间。比赛中他的主要职责是监督记录台工作人员的工作，并协助裁判员使比赛顺利进行。
一致性	N/A	裁判员在整场比赛中对所有情况做出的判罚和解释自始至终都相同。
接触犯规	N/A	一名队员接触另一名队员并致使其不利的侵人犯规。
控制球	COB	球队控制球开始于该队一名队员正持有或运着一个活球，或者在掷球入界情况下可处理活球时。控制球一直持续到一次投篮发生，裁判员鸣哨，或对方队员取得控制球。一名队员控制球指的是当他正持有或运着一个活球，或者掷球入界或罚球情况下可处理一个活球时。
可纠正失误	CE	如果在下列情况中某条规则被无意地忽视了，裁判员可纠正该失误： • 判给不应得的罚球。 • 没有判给应得的罚球。 • 不正确地判给或取消得分。 • 允许不该罚球的队员执行罚球。
覆盖	CG	两名/三名裁判员对比赛的视野；良好的视野覆盖意味着裁判员把所有有球和无球的队员尽收眼底。

TERM	ABBR	EXPLANATION
Crew Chief	CC	The Crew Chief (CC) is generally the more senior and/or experienced of the two/three referees. The crew chief's duties are the same as the umpire(s) except that the crew chief: 1. Initiates the start of the game and of each quarter. 2. Inspects and approves all equipment to be used in the game 3. Has the power to make the final decision on any point not specifically covered in the rules.
Cross Step	CS	When play starts to progress in one direction and designated referee takes steps in the opposite direction. This adjustment can be done in all positions as Lead, Trail & Centre.
Cylinder (Principle)	CP	The imaginary vertical extension of a player. Players are entitled to occupy a spot on the floor and also the cylinder above them (i.e. they can jump straight up without giving up position).

Dead Ball	DB	The ball becomes dead when:
		1. Any field goal or free throw is made.
		2. A referee blows the whistle while the ball is live.
		3. It is apparent that the ball will not enter the basket on a free throw which is to be followed by:
		  3.1 Another free throw(s).
		  3.2 A further penalty (free throw(s) and/or possession).
		4. The game clock signal sounds for the end of the quarter.
		5. The shot clock signal sounds while a team is in control of the ball.

Dead Ball Officiating	DBO	Refers to any actions that take place after the referee makes the call and the ball becomes live again. Dead-ball officiating is primarily proactive and requires that the (two) other passive referee(s) become active during the dead ball period.
Disqualification	DQ	A disqualifying foul is any flagrant unsportsmanlike action by a player or team bench personnel.

术语	缩写	解释
主裁判员	CC	主裁判（CC）通常是2人或3人执裁团队中资历更丰富的。主裁判的职责与副裁判相同，除了： 1. 执行比赛开场跳球和其他每一节的开始掷球入界。 2. 检查和批准在比赛中使用的所有器材。 3. 有权对规则中未明确规定的任何事项做出决定。
交叉步	CS	在自己主要责任区的裁判员向比赛发展方向的反方向做出的移动称为交叉步，前导、追踪和中央裁判都会做出这样的调整。
圆柱体（垂直原则）	CP	队员所占据的假想的垂直空间，每一名队员都有权占据场上任何位置（圆柱体）。这个原则保护队员所占据的地面空间和垂直起跳时的上方空间。
死球	DB	球成死球，当： 1. 任何投篮或罚球中篮时。 2. 活球时，裁判员鸣哨。 3. 在一次罚球明显不会中篮，且罚球后有： ——另一次或多次罚球时。 ——进一步罚则（罚球和/或掷球入界）时。 4. 比赛计时钟信号响以结束一切或决胜期时。 5. 某队控制球，进攻时钟信号响时。
执裁死球情况	DBO	指的是裁判员做出宣判后到球再次成为活球之前发生的任何情况，执裁死球情况主要是两名非宣判裁判需要在死球期间保持警惕和关注。
取消比赛资格	DQ	队员或球队席人员的任何恶劣的违反体育运动精神的行为是取消比赛资格的犯规。

TERM	ABBR	EXPLANATION
Double Dribble	DD	An illegal dribble when a player discontinues the dribble action by allowing the ball to touch both hands on a dribble or allowing the ball to come to rest in one hand and then proceeds to dribble again.
Double Foul	DOF	A double foul is a situation in which 2 opponents commit personal or unsportsmanlike/disqualifying fouls on each other at approximately the same time. To consider 2 fouls as a double foul the following conditions must apply: • Both fouls are player fouls. • Both fouls involve physical contact • Both fouls are between the same 2 opponents fouling each other. • Both fouls are either 2 personal or any combination of unsportsmanlike and disqualifying fouls.
Double Whistle	DW	When two referees simultaneously blow their whistles.
Dribble	DR	A dribble is the movement of a live ball caused by a player in control of that ball who throws, taps, rolls the ball on the floor.
Dual Coverage	DUCE	Area of responsibility and actions that two referees have overlapping primary responsibilities on the same area or play.
Edge of the Play	EPL	In Lead position it is crucial to adjust your positioning with the ball and to be in line with outside players in order to maintain the players in the field of vision and open look. When on the edge of the play, a referee is normally able to see more players and anticipate better next play situations to come. This position is linked with the term "45° angle".
Eight (8) Seconds Violation	8S	When a team gains new possession of the ball in their backcourt, it has eight seconds to advance the ball over the centre line.
Ejection	N/A	When a referee orders a player off the court for a disqualifying foul or for a second technical or unsportsmanlike foul on the same player.

术语	缩写	解释
两次运球	DD	非法运球，当队员双手同时触及球或允许球在一手或双手中停留后再次开始一次运球。
双方犯规	DOF	双方犯规是两名互为对方的队员大约同时相互发生侵人犯规或违反体育运动精神犯规/取消比赛资格犯规的情况。将两个犯规视为一起双方犯规，下列条件是必须的： • 两个犯规都是队员犯规。 • 两个犯规都包含身体接触。 • 两个犯规是比赛双方两名队员之间的相互犯规。 • 两个犯规是两个侵人犯规或任何违反体育运动精神的犯规和取消比赛资格的犯规的组合。
双哨	DW	两名裁判员同时鸣哨。
运球	DR	运球是指一名队员控制一个活球的一系列动作：将球在地面上掷、拍、滚、运或将球弹在地面上。
共管区	DUCE	两名裁判员应共同负责和观察比赛情况的责任区，该责任区同时是两名裁判员的主要责任区。
比赛边缘	EPL	对于前导裁判而言，根据球的位置调整站位，与外侧队员平行极其重要，这样做是为了获取观察队员的视野和开角，在比赛边缘站位通常能够使裁判员看到更多的队员并更好地预判下一个攻防矛盾情况，这种站位与术语"45°"息息相关。
8秒违例	8S	在后场获得一次新的球权的球队必须在8秒内使球进入该队的前场。
驱逐	N/A	当一名队员发生了一起取消比赛资格的犯规或是第二次技术犯规/违反体育运动精神的犯规时，该队员应离开比赛场地。

TERM	ABBR	EXPLANATION
Elbowing	ELW	Any hit or contact made with the elbow that imply a foul. Also - An action of excessive swinging of elbows by and offensive player with the ball (without contact).
End Of the Game	EOG	End of the Game
End Of the Quarter	EOQ	End of the Quarter
Endline (Baseline)	N/A	The boundary lines marking both ends of the playing area. The line itself is considered to be out-of-bounds. In US basketball, they use the "baseline" term.
Extended Coverage	EXCE	At the highest level of officiating, a referee has to be able to extend coverage on two different play situations at the same time.
Fake (Basketball)	N/A	Normally an offensive manoeuvre when an offensive player fakes motion in one direction to draw a defensive player that way and then attempts to move past the defence in the other direction.
Fake (Refereeing)	FK	Fake (Refereeing) is any action where a player pretends being fouled or makes theatrical exaggerated movements in order to create an opinion of being fouled and therefore gaining an unfair advantage. Examples of faking are: falling backwards, falling down, moving the head backwards, etc. simulating contact by an opponent without actually being touched, or being contacted only in a marginal way (see "Flop").
Fantasy Call (Phantom Call)	FAC	Describes the situation when a referee makes a call for foul and actually there was not even contact on the play (problem with selfdiscipline / "I don't see, I don't call"). This is different than Marginal Contact that is incorrectly called as a foul (problem with criteria).
Fast Break	FB	A quick change of the direction of the ball as the defensive team gains possession of the ball through a steal, rebound, violation or made shot and quickly attacks to the other end of the court hoping to gain numerical or positional advantage over the other team and a resultant high percentage shot.

术语	缩写	解释
肘击	ELW	任何以肘部造成的击打或接触都会导致一起犯规。同样也指有球的进攻队员过分挥肘的动作（无接触）。
比赛末	EOG	比赛结束时。
节末	EOQ	单节结束时。
端线（底线）	N/A	比赛场地两端标出的界线。这些线不是比赛场地的部分。在美国篮球中，他们被称为"底线"。
延伸区域	EXCE	在最高级别的执裁工作中，一名裁判员必须有能力覆盖到延伸区域并同时观察到两个不同的比赛情况。
假动作（篮球技术）	N/A	一般来说是进攻队员为了吸引防守队员向一个方向移动而利用假动作做出的技术，其目的是为了向另一个方向突破防守。
骗取犯规（执裁）	FK	骗取犯规是一名队员为了假装被犯规或使用戏剧性的夸张动作来制造被犯规的假象而从中获取不正当利益。骗取犯规如：身体向后移动、倒地，头部向后移动等。在实际上没有与对手发生接触的情况下制造出被接触的假象或是仅仅与对手发生了附带接触的话请参照"假摔"。
猜判	FAC	所描述的情况指的是裁判员做出了犯规的宣判，可事实上该情况甚至没有身体接触（自律的问题/"我没看到就不吹"）。这种情况不同于因尺度理解问题而错误地把附带接触宣判成了犯规。
快攻	FB	快攻指的是防守队通过抢断、篮板球、违例或球中篮后而控球并快速转换进攻方向，并试图迅速进攻至球场另一端以获取最大化进攻队员数量优势和位置优势的同时得到高命中率的得分机会。

TERM	ABBR	EXPLANATION
Feel for the Game	N/A	The referee's ability to be sense what's going on the court: are tempers getting high; is the pace fast; is there too much contact occurring, etc.? A referee with a good feel for the game is in the best position to maintain game control.
Fighting	FGT	Fighting is physical interaction between 2 or more opponents (players and/or team bench personnel).
Five (5) Fouls	5F	A player who has committed 5 fouls shall be informed by a referee and must leave the game immediately and must be substituted within 30 seconds.
Five (5) Seconds Violation	5S	Once a player has the ball at disposal for a throw-in or a free throw, he/she has five seconds to release the ball. Also when a closely guarded player is in control of the ball, he/she has five seconds to pass, shoot or dribble - not to do so is a violation. A closely guarded player who is dribbling is not subject to a five second count.
Flagrant Foul	FF	May be a personal or technical foul. It is always unsportsmanlike and may or may not be intentional. If personal, it involves violent or savage contact, such as striking with the fist or elbow, kicking, kneeing, or running under a player who is in the air, or crouching or hipping in a manner which might cause severe injury to an opponent. If it is a non-contact foul, it involves extreme and sometimes persistent vulgar and/or abusive conduct.
Flop (Refereeing)	FL	Any fake, pretend, or exaggerated action by a player with/without the ball - e.g. falling backwards, falling down, throwing the head, etc. - simulating contact by an opponent in an unnatural manner without actually being touched, or being contacted in only a marginal way.
Foot (Kick) Violation	FVI	A player shall not run with the ball, deliberately kick or block it with any part of the leg or strike it with the fist. However, to accidentally come into contact with or touch the ball with any part of the leg is not a violation. (Deliberate Foot Ball).
Foul	N/A	A foul is an infraction of the rules concerning illegal personal contact with an opponent and/or unsportsmanlike behaviour.

术语	缩写	解释
对比赛的感觉	N/A	指的是裁判员对比赛中所发生一切的感觉：火药味浓郁、节奏加快、太多身体接触等情况。一名对比赛有良好感觉的裁判员能够胜任对比赛的控制和管理。
打架	FGT	打架是两名或者多名互为对方队的人员（队员和球队席人员）之间的肢体冲突。
五次犯规	5F	一名队员已经发生了5次犯规，裁判员应通知其本人，他必须立即离开比赛，并且必须在30秒内被替换。
五秒违例	5S	在掷球入界或罚球情况时可处理球的队员有5秒的时间使球离手。同样的对于一名持球的被严密防守的队员而言，他有5秒可以传球、投篮或者运球，否则则是一起违例。一名被严密防守的运球队员不适用于5秒计算。
恶意犯规	FF	可能是侵人或者技术犯规。但这样的犯规一定是违反体育运动精神的（无论故意与否）。如果是侵人犯规，则包括了暴力或野蛮的接触，比如拳击、肘击、踢、膝顶、跑向空中队员下方或以下蹲、跨步顶撞等这些可能造成对手严重受伤的方式。如果是非接触犯规，则包括了极端的和持续不断的粗俗低劣的语言攻击。
假摔	FL	任何有球或无球队员虚假、假装或者夸张的行为，比如向后退步、倒地、猛烈仰头等试图以对手与自身接触而伪造出的非自然结果（无接触或轻微接触都是假摔）。
脚（踢）球违例	FVI	队员不能带球跑，故意踢或者用腿的任何部分阻挡球或用拳击球。然而球意外地接触到腿的任何部分或腿的任何部分意外接触到球不是违例。
犯规	N/A	犯规是对规则的违反，含有与对方队员的非法身体接触或违反体育运动精神的举止。

TERM	ABBR	EXPLANATION
Foul Lane	N/A	The restricted area at both ends of the court circumscribed by the foul line, foul lanes and baselines. Also called the "key" or "paint".
Foul not in Act of shooting	FNAOS	When a player is illegally contacted by the defence and foul is called, but not AOS (also term "Foul on floor").
Fouled in Act of Shooting (AOS)	FAOS	FAOS When a player is illegally contacted by the defence when attempting a shot or during the contious motion.
Free Throw Line Extended	FTEX	This imaginary line represents the extension of the free throw line across the width of the court. Most coaches use it to establish defensive coaching guidelines. When the ball is above the free throw line extended a certain guideline applies. When the ball is below it another guideline applies. It is also used as a reference for offensive player alignment. FTEX is also a set-up (basic) position for the Centre on the court.
Free Throw(s)	FT	A free throw is an opportunity given to a player to score 1 point, uncontested, from a position behind the free-throw line and inside the semi-circle.
Freedom of Movement	FOM	A cardinal term also in the rules denoting the ability of a player to move from one spot on the court to another without being unduly hindered. If contact caused by a player in any way restricts the freedom of movement of an opponent, such a contact is a foul.
Freeze	N/A	In the case of simultaneous whistles, the referee who feels he/she is in the least advantageous position to make the call (usually the referee furthest away from the incident) should remain stationary momentarily (freeze) in order to let his/her partner move toward the incident and begin administering the situation.
Frontcourt	FC	A team's frontcourt consists of the opponents' basket, the inbounds part of the backboard and that part of the playing court limited by the endline behind the opponents' basket, the sidelines and the inner edge of the centre line nearest to the opponents' basket.

术语	缩写	解释
限制区	N/A	球场两侧的限制区域由罚球线、限制区线和端线组成。也被称为关键区或油漆区。
非投篮犯规	FNAOS	当一名未做投篮尝试的队员遭到防守队员非法接触并吹罚犯规。
投篮犯规	FAOS	当一名正在做投篮尝试的队员遭到防守队员非法接触并吹罚犯规。
罚球线延长线	FTEX	这条假想的线代表着场地两边罚球线的延长线。多数教练员利用该线布置防守战术。当球在罚球线延长线上方时是一种战术，球在罚球线下方时又是一种战术。该线同样被用作进攻队员的站位布置。罚球线延长线也是中央裁判在场上的初始落位点。
罚球	FT	一次罚球是给予一名队员从罚球线后的半圆内的位置上，在无争抢的情况下得一分的机会。
自由移动	FOM	该词汇在规则中同样是重要术语。阐述的是一名队员在场上可以从一处移动到另一处，期间不宜受到过度阻碍或接触。如果对手这样的接触限制了一名队员的自由移动的话，该接触就是一起犯规。
静立	N/A	在同时鸣哨的情况中感到自己的宣判不一定比同伴（通常是离比赛情况最远的那名裁判员）更有说服力或站位更佳的话，应当保持静止站立以便让同伴移动并管理该比赛情况。
前场	FC	某队的前场是由对方的球篮、篮板的界内部分以及对方球篮后面的端线、两条边线和距离对方球篮最近的中线内沿所界定的比赛场地部分组成。

TERM	ABBR	EXPLANATION
Game Control	GC	A referee is said to be in control of a game when the game is operating smoothly under the rules as intended and, as well as, the rules of sportsmanship being rigidly but fairly enforced. This is different than Game Management.
Game Flow	GF	The speed or tempo at which the game is being played. This is determined by the two contesting teams and the referees should attempt as much as possible not to interrupt this flow.
Game Saver	GS	An important and correct decision made by a referee irrespective to his/her position or area of responsibility at the end of a game that is crucial to protecting the game's integrity (literally "saves the game"), and if otherwise not made, could create a situation whereby the team that deserves to win the game, may not.
Giving Help	GH	Referee who offers assistance outside his/her primary and makes a correct call after allowing his/her partner to make the call in his/her primary.
Goal (field goal)	FG	A goal is made when a live ball enters the basket from above and remains within or passes through the basket. The ball is considered to be within the basket when the slightest part of the ball is within and below the level of the ring.
Goaltending	GT	Goaltending occurs during a shot for a field goal when a player touches the ball while it is completely above the level of the ring and: • It is on its downward flight to the basket, or • After it has touched the backboard.
Hand Checking	HC	Hand Checking / Illegal use of the hand(s) or extended arm(s) occurs when the defensive player is in a guarding position and his/her hand(s) or arm(s) is placed upon and remains in contact with an opponent with or without the ball, to impede opponent's progress.
Held Ball	HB	A held ball occurs when one or more players from opposing teams have one or both hands firmly on the ball so that neither player can gain control without undue roughness.

术语	缩写	解释
比赛控制	GC	当一名裁判员在既定的规则下使比赛流畅地进行，同时严格执行符合体育运动精神的规定，但不是执行强制性公平时，他被认为是掌控了一场比赛。这不同于比赛管理。
比赛流畅性	GF	比赛在何种速度和节奏下进行，这取决于竞赛双方，同时取决于应当尽可能少打断比赛流畅性的裁判员们。
拯救比赛的判罚	GS	无论自己的站位和职责区在哪里，裁判员在比赛终了时刻所做出的重要和正确的决定都必须捍卫比赛的公平和公正（拯救比赛判罚），这是极为重要的，如果没有做到这一点，那么原本应当获得比赛胜利的球队也许得到了相反的结果。
给予帮助	GH	一名裁判员只有在允许其同伴在其主要责任区内做出宣判的前提下才可以在他自己的主要责任区外做出正确判罚。
球中篮	FG	当活球从上方进入球篮并停留在球篮内或穿过球篮是球中篮，当有极少部分的球体在篮圈中并在篮圈水平面以下时就认为球在球篮中。
干涉得分	GT	干涉得分发生在一次投篮中，当一名队员接触完全在篮圈水平面之上的球时： • 球是下落飞向球篮中，或 • 在球已碰击篮板后。
用手推挡	HC	当防守队员处于防守位置并且其手或手臂放置在持球或不持球的对方队员身上，并保持接触以阻碍其前进就发生了非法用手或非法伸展手臂。
争球	HB	当双方球队各有一名或多名队员有一手或两手紧握在球上，以至不采用粗野动作任一队员就不能获得控制球时，一次争球发生。

TERM	ABBR	EXPLANATION
Help Side	HSB	The half of the front court opposite to where the ball is located (taken from an imaginary line extending from the ring, through the top of the key to the centre jump circle).
Holding	HOL	Holding is illegal personal contact with an opponent that interferes with opponent´s freedom of movement. This contact (holding) can occur with any part of the body.
Hooking	HOK	When an offensive player "hooks" or wraps an arm or an elbow around a defensive player in order to prevent the defender from playing legal defence.
Illegal Dribble	IDR	A violation made by the dribbler either carrying the ball or making a double dribble.
Illegal Use of Hands	IUH	Illegally using the hands to impede the progress of an opposition player. Normally this foul is made on a dribbler and entails the defence hacking the arms of the dribbler in an attempt to bat the ball away.
Image of the Referee	IOR	How the referee is perceived by others. For example, if the referee is sloppy looking, the image they create may bias players and coaches to expect they will referee sloppily. A top referee's image is "Strong, Decisive & Approachable".
Individual Officiating Techniques	IOT	The technical aspects of individual refereeing how to referee the play using proper techniques such as Distance & Stationary, Refereeing the Defence, Active Mindset, "Staying with the play", Adjustment to maintain Open Angle, etc.
Infraction	N/A	Literally any infraction is a contravention of the rules. e.g. fouls(technical and contact) and violations. However, normally infractions refer to just violations (i.e. three seconds, travelling etc.).
Inside-Out (Angle)	IN-O	This generally refers to the Lead referee who may not be on the edge of the play and instead is looking from the Inside-Out, instead of refereeing at a 45 degree angle with as many players as possible within the field of vision.

术语	缩写	解释
协助侧	HSB	位于前场有球侧的对面（连接球篮和中圈顶弧的假想线上）。
拉人	HOL	拉人是干扰对方队员移动自由的非法身体接触。这种接触（拉人）可能发生在身体的任何部位。
钩人	HOK	进攻队员为了获得不公正的利益，用手臂或肘"勾住"或缠绕防守队员以致对方无法正常且合法防守。
非法运球	IDR	运球队员因携带球或两次运球而造成的违例。
非法用手	IUH	非法用手指的是用手阻碍对手的行进。一般这样的犯规发生在运球队员身上，该规则的目的是为了限制防守队员在试图断球的过程中不顾后果地拍击运球队员的手臂。
裁判形象	IOR	即人们眼中的裁判员。如果裁判员看上去是懒散的，那么队员们和教练们都会带有偏见地认为你会懒散地执裁。顶尖裁判员的形象应当是"强有力，坚决却平易近人"。
个人执裁技术	IOT	指的是裁判员通过应用自己的技术水平去恰当执裁，比如距离和保持静止、执裁防守、动态思维、看完整比赛情况、调节、保持开角等。
违犯	N/A	简单来说，违犯就是对规则的违反。如：犯规（技术或带身体接触的）和违例。然而，违犯通常只指违例（如：3秒、带球走等）。
内向外观察（角度）	IN–O	通常指的是前导裁判所占的位置看不到边缘的比赛情况，便以"内向外"的角度去观察比赛情况，而不是以常规的45°去观察尽量多的队员。

TERM	ABBR	EXPLANATION
Instant Replay System	IRS	Refers to a video replay system what is possible to use in designated play situations. The IRS review will be conducted by the referees. If the call and the decision of the referees is subject to the IRS review, that initial decision must be shown by the referees on the playing court. Following the IRS review the initial decision of the referee(s) can be corrected only if the IRS review provides the referees with clear and conclusive visual evidence for the correction.
Interpretation of the Rules	N/A	Good refereeing requires that a referee does not apply the rules literally (i.e. contact is not allowed), but rather, judges each situation in regards to its effect on the play, i.e. interpreting the rules by their spirit and intention.
Interval (of Play)	IOP	There shall be an interval of play of 20 minutes before the game is scheduled to begin. There shall be intervals of play of 2 minutes between the first and second quarter (first half), between the third and fourth quarter (second half) and before each overtime. There shall be a half-time interval of play of 15 minutes. During an interval of play, all team members entitled to play are considered as players.
Jab (handchecking)	JAB	To repeatedly touch or 'jab' an opponent with or without the ball is a foul, as it may lead to rough play.
Judgement	N/A	The ability of a referee to look at each situation as it arises and make a decision based on its effect or non-effect on play and to act accordingly.
Jump Ball (Situation)	JB	A jump ball occurs when a referee tosses the ball in the centre circle between any 2 opponents at the beginning of the first quarter. Can also refer to a "jump ball situation."
Last Shot	LS	Refers to the play when team has a new control of the ball and the game clock shows 24.0 seconds or less, meaning it is possible that the quarter will end with that team possession.
Last 2 minutes of the game	L2M	Refers to the last 2 minutes of the fourth quarter and overtime.

术语	缩写	解释
即时回放系统	IRS	指在特定的比赛情况中可以使用的录像回放系统，即时回放系统仅供裁判员们使用。如裁判员的判罚或决定属于即时回放系统可回放范围内，那么裁判员必须在比赛场上做出初判。在即时回放系统回放之后，只有在即时回放系统回放能够提供给裁判员清晰准确的图像证据前提下，裁判员才可以改正初判。
规则解释	N/A	优秀的执裁要求裁判员不能单从字面理解规则（如：不允许任何接触），而是判断每一个比赛情况是否会因接触而受到影响，如：根据精神和意图解释规则。
比赛休息期间	IOP	在预定的比赛开始之前，应有20分钟的比赛休息期间。 在第1节和第2节（上半时）之间，第3节和第4节（下半时）之间，以及每一决胜期之前，应有2分钟的比赛休息期间。 两个半时之间的比赛休息期间应是15分钟。在比赛休息期间，所有有资格参赛的球队成员，被认为是队员。
戳刺（用手推挡）	JAB	反复地触及或"戳刺"持球或不持球的对方队员是犯规，因为这可能会导致粗暴的比赛。
判断	N/A	裁判员根据每个比赛情况的发展和是否对比赛情况造成影响做出宣判与否的能力。
跳球（情况）	JB	在第1节开始时，一名裁判员在中圈、在任何两名互为对方的队员之间将球抛起，一次跳球发生。这同样指"跳球情况"。
最后一攻	LS	在单节比赛计时钟显示24（或少于24）秒时某队获得了一个新的球权，意味着这次进攻可能是该节该队的最后一攻。
比赛的最后2分钟	L2M	指的是第4节或决胜期的最后2分钟。

TERM	ABBR	EXPLANATION
Lead (Referee)	L	The Lead (2PO/3PO) is the referee who leads the play up the court and whose responsibility includes coverage along the endline at the attacking end of the court.
Legal Guarding Position	LGP	A defensive player has established an initial legal guarding position when: • player is facing his/her opponent, and • player has both feet on the floor.
Line Up	N/A	During a foul shot players "line up" on either side of the foul lane.
Live Ball	LB	The ball becomes live when: 1. During the jump ball, the ball leaves the hand(s) of the referee on the toss. 2. During a free throw, the ball is at the disposal of the free-throw shooter. 3. During a throw-in, the ball is at the disposal of the player taking the throw-in.
Loose Ball	LOB	When a live ball is not in possession of a player but is rolling or bouncing on the floor as players from both sides seek to gain control or as in a rebounding situation. Team control does not change until the opposition gains control, meaning for example, a shot clock violation can occur while the ball is loose.
Manufactured (Shot)	MS	Anytime that a player who is not in act of shooting when illegalcontact occurs, but after the contact starts an AOS movement hoping to have free throws awarded.
Marginal Contact	MC	Although basketball is a non-contact sport it is virtually impossible for players to move around the court without contacting each other. If the contact is seen to affect the play, then a foul should be called. Other contact which has no effect on the play is deemed marginal and can be ignored.
Mechanics	MEC	The technical aspects of refereeing i.e. how referees move, coverage, signals, administration of free throws, jump ball situations, throw-ins, etc…

术语	缩写	解释
前导裁判（裁判）	L	前导裁判（2人／3人执裁）是比赛过程中最先到达进攻方向前场并负责接管端线周边比赛情况的裁判员。
合理的防守位置	LGP	当一名防守队员： • 面对对手，并且 • 双脚着地时。 他就占据了最初的合法防守位置。
列队占位	N/A	在一次罚球期间，非罚球队员"列队占位"于限制区两侧。
活球	LB	球成活球，当： 1. 跳球中，球离开主裁判员抛球的手时。 2. 罚球中，罚球队员可处理球时。 3. 掷球入界中，掷球入界队员可处理球时。
失去控球	LOB	此状态指的是当一个不属于任一队控制的活球在球场上滚动或反弹时，或在一起篮板球情况中双方队员都试图去获得控制球时。而在对手获得控制球之前，原控制球队不失去控球，比如：无队员持球状态时可能发生一起进攻时间违例。
制造（投篮动作）	MS	在发生犯规时被犯规队员并非在做投篮动作，但在接触发生后他开始了一次投篮动作以希望获取罚球。
附带接触	MC	虽然篮球是一项无身体接触的运动，但场上不断移动的队员之间不发生身体接触是不可能的。如果比赛因接触而受到影响，则应宣判犯规。那些对比赛并不产生影响的身体接触应被视为是附带的并可以被忽略。
裁判法	MEC	执裁方面的技术组成，如：裁判员的移动、责任区、手势、罚球的管理、跳球情况、掷球入界等。

TERM	ABBR	EXPLANATION
Media Time-Out(s)	MTO	The organising body of the competition may decide for itself whether media time-outs shall be applied and, if so, of what duration (e.g. 60, 75, 90 or 100 seconds).
No-Call	NC	Some of the best decisions a referee may make involve in refraining from blowing the whistle, when he/she judges a potential foul or violation does not contravene the spirit and intent of the rules.
Non-Active Referee	NAR	The referee who is not administrating free throw or a throw-in, or to not tossing the ball during the jump ball in the start of the game.
Obvious Play	OP	Plays that are clearly visible to most of the participants in the game, including referees, coaches, players and spectators. Referees must be correct in these type of situations 100% of the time with no room for error.
Off the Ball	OFB	Concerns all aspects of play not directly involving the player with the ball and players closely adjacent to them.
Offensive End	N/A	The end of the court to which a team attacks and attempts to score a basket (their front court).
Official Basketball Rules Interpretations	OBRI	A document that FIBA publishes, which includes all official interpretations defined by FIBA.
Open Angle	OA	Clear view of the action in a referee's primary / secondary coverage area. Never leave an open look.
Opposite Side Interpretations	OPS	This refers to the side of the playing court which is furthest away from the scorer's table.
Out-of Bounds	OOB	That area outside of the playing court – radiating out from and including the boundary lines of the court.
Outside-In (Angle)	O-IN	The preferred position of the Lead referee who is standing at a 45 degree angle and has as many players as possible within the field of vision.
Palming (the ball)	PLM	See: carrying the ball.

术语	缩写	解释
媒体暂停	MTO	竞赛组织部门可自行决定是否运用媒体暂停，如运用，并决定何种持续时间（60秒、75秒、90秒或100秒）。
不宣判	NC	当裁判员判断一起可能发生的犯规或违例并不违背规则的精神和意图时，一些情况下他所做出的最佳决定便是不以鸣哨打断比赛。这就叫不宣判。
非执行裁判	NAR	没有在管理罚球或掷球入界，也没有执行开场跳球的裁判员。
明显的情况	OP	比赛中对多数观看者而言都是清晰可见的情况，包括裁判员、教练、队员和观众。裁判员对此类情况必须做到100%准确无误，不留错误的余地。
无球情况	OFB	指的是非持球队员和持球队员邻近周边队员的比赛情况。
进攻端	N/A	某队进攻方向或试图得分的半场(即他们的前场)。
篮球规则解释	OBRI	国际篮联颁布的文件之一，包含国际篮联所有的官方规则解释。
开角	OA	裁判员在自己的主要/次要责任区内能看清比赛情况的视野。应始终寻找开角。
对侧	OPS	指远离记录台的场地一侧。
出界	OOB	球场地面之外的部分——用界线来区分界内界外，界线属于界外。
外向内观察（角度）	O-IN	前导裁判的最佳占位应是45°，那样的话他的视野可以看到最多的队员。
翻腕	PLM	见：携带球。

TERM	ABBR	EXPLANATION
Pass	N/A	A method of moving the ball by throwing it from one offensive player to another.
Pass-Off	POFF	A situation where a player has started the AOS and a foul is called, but does not continue shooting motion and ends up passing to a teammate. This is considered a personal foul and not AOS foul.
Patienced Whistle	PW	When referee is capable to process the entire play (start/middle/end) before making a call.
Peripheral Vision	PV	To see widely to either side while looking straight ahead.
Personal Foul	PF	A personal foul is a player's illegal contact with an opponent, whether the ball is live or dead.
Phantom Call (Fantasy Call)	FAC	Describes the situation when a referee makes a call for foul and actually there was not even contact on the play (problem with selfdiscipline / "I don't see, I don't call"). This is different than Marginal Contact that is incorrectly called as a foul (problem with criteria).
Pick	SC	An offensive screen.
Pivot Foot	PF	When a player is in possession of the ball and is not dribbling he/she is allowed to rotate around one foot providing that this foot remains on the same spot on the floor – thus a pivot foot.
Player	N/A	During playing time, a team member is a player when he/she is on the playing court and is entitled to play.
Pre-Game Conference	PGC	Before the start of important contests it is necessary for the referees to meet together to familiarise themselves and talk about their working mechanics and preparations for the game.
Pre-Game Routines	N/A	The routine the referees go through prior to the actual commencement of the game. This includes checking the scoresheet, making sure the timer understands the timing regulations of that particular contest, etc.
Preventative Officiating	PRO	Refers to actions by referees who prevent problems from occurring by communicating with players and/or coaches. It can happen during live ball (post, perimeter play) as well as during dead ball.

术语	缩写	解释
传球	N/A	进攻队员用来将球掷向另一名队员以移动球的方式。
以传球收尾	POFF	当一名队员正在做投篮动作时遭到犯规，而他却停止投篮动作，最终传球给队友。这样的情况将被判为对非投篮动作的犯规。
耐心哨	PW	裁判员在确定宣判前看清并分析了整个过程（开始/发展/结束）。
余光视野	PV	在主要视野看着正前方的同时放宽视野至周边一侧。
侵人犯规	PF	侵人犯规是：无论在活球或死球的情况下，攻守双方队员发生的非法身体接触的犯规。
猜判	FAC	所描述的情况指的是裁判员做出了犯规的宣判，可事实上该情况甚至没有身体接触（自律的问题／"我没看到就不吹"）。这种情况不同于因尺度理解问题而错误地把附带接触宣判成了犯规。
掩护	SC	一起进攻队掩护。
中枢脚	PF	当一名队员持着一个活球时，他可以旋转单脚，只要该脚在原地旋转——这就是中枢脚。
队员	N/A	在比赛时间内，一名球队成员在比赛场地上，并且有资格参赛时，是一名队员。
赛前准备会	PGC	在重要的比赛开始之前，裁判员们会晤并相互熟悉是完全有必要的，他们也应该讨论比赛中将应用到的裁判法和事先准备好的内容。
赛前的例行流程	N/A	这些例行流程都是裁判员应当在赛前就完成的。包括检查记录表，确保计时员知晓该场比赛特殊情况下的计时方法等等。
预见性执裁	PRO	裁判员在有些问题发生之前就已经和队员以及教练员沟通过。这些问题情况可能发生在活球期间（单打，中距离突破），也可能发生在死球期间。

TERM	ABBR	EXPLANATION
Primary (Coverage)	PCE	Area of responsibility and actions that referee has to be able to cover always.
Push-Off	PO	When an offensive player 'pushes off' to prevent the defensive player from playing or attempting to play the ball, or to create more space for himself.
Pushing	PU	Pushing is illegal personal contact with any part of the body where a player forcibly moves or attempts to move an opponent with or without the ball.
Quick Whistle	QW	When referee is not capable to process the entire play before making a call. Sometimes quick whistles lead to unnecessary calls.
Rebound	RB	On a missed shot, the resultant contest between the two teams to gain possession of the ball is known as rebounding (the ball rebounds off the ring or backboard). Thus, to get a rebound means to secure the ball after a missed shot.
Rectangle	RC	Refers to the frontcourt, which has been divided into 6 parts for the purpose of defining areas of responsibility.
Ref	N/A	Short for referee
Referee	REF	Generally, the term used for two/three referees working a game.
Referees	N/A	The referees shall be a crew chief and 1 or 2 umpire(s). They shall be assisted by the table officials and by a commissioner, if present.
Referee Instructor	RI	The referee instructor is a person who has good knowledge in teaching & learning, basketball and refereeing. FIBA has certified and trained Referee Instructors.
Refereeing Defence	RD	The priority when refereeing on ball is to focus the attention on the illegality of the defensive player while keeping the offensive player with the ball in your field of vision.
Regular call	RC	Considered to be normal call by designated referee (no assistance).
Ring	N/A	The metal circumference of the basket or hoop the ball must pass through in order to record a score.

术语	缩写	解释
主要（责任区）	PCE	裁判员必须总是能够覆盖到的责任区和比赛情况。
推开	PO	进攻队员为了阻止防守队员的防守或试图抢球，或为了在他和防守队员之间创造更大的空间而"推开"防守队员。
推人	PU	推人是队员用身体的任何部位强行移动或试图移动有球或无球的对方队员时发生的非法身体接触。
过快鸣哨	QW	裁判员在宣判前没有分析整个比赛片段。有时这样的宣判是毫无必要的。
篮板球	RB	在一次球未中篮后，双方队员为了夺取控制球的过程被称为抢篮板球（球通过篮圈或篮板反弹）。所以，抢到篮板球就是在球未中篮后拿到控制球。
矩形区域	RC	在前场，被划分为 6 片不同责任区的整块区域被称为"矩形区"。
裁判员	N/A	裁判员的缩写。
裁判员	REF	通常来说，此术语用于 2 人 / 3 人执裁中。
裁判团队	N/A	裁判团应由 1 名主裁判和 1 名或者 2 名副裁判组成，记录台人员或到场的技术代表应协助他们。
裁判讲师	RI	裁判讲师是具有良好的教与学、篮球知识和执裁理论的人。国际篮联已经认证和培训了一批裁判讲师。
执裁防守	RD	执裁有球情况时最重要的是注意观察防守队员的动作合法性，同时视野不离持球的进攻队员。
常规宣判	RC	视为指定裁判员所做出的普通宣判（无需协助）。
球篮	N/A	为了得分而使球必须穿过的圆形的金属篮状体。

FIBA REFEREES MANUAL

TERM	ABBR	EXPLANATION
Rotation	ROT	This refers to a situation when the movement/location of the ball causes the Lead to initiate a change of position or "rotation" to the ball side in the frontcourt. The trigger for Lead to rotate is when ball moves to Centre side (weak side) and stay there. A change in position by Lead affects changes in position by Centre (to Trail) and Trail (to Centre).
Scan (the Paint)	SPA	When Lead rotates on the baseline, he needs to scan the paint for illegal off-ball activities or if no players, next action area.
Score	FG	To make a basket or free throw. It can also refer to the point totals of both teams – as in the score of the game was 50 to 47.
Scorer	SR	The scorer shall keep a record of the scoresheet according to the basketball rules.
Scoresheet	SS	The official record of the game details, which is kept throughout the game. The scoresheet records a running tally of the team and individual scores and fouls.
Screening	SC	Screening is an attempt to delay or prevent an opponent without the ball from reaching a desired position on the playing court.
Secondary (Coverage)	SCE	Area of responsibility and actions that referee is able to cover after ensuring that primary coverage is covered.
Self-Evaluation	SEF	The process of evaluation of one's own performance.
Selling the Call	STC	Placing emphasis on a call with louder voice and whistle and slightly more demonstrative signals. It should happen only in close calls in order to help the call gain acceptance.
Semi-Circle (No-Charge)	NCSC	The no-charge semi-circle areas are drawn on the playing court for the purpose of designating a specific area for the interpretation of charge/block situations under the basket. The no-charge semi-circle lines are part of the no-charge semi-circle areas.
Shot	N/A	An attempt at the basket.

术语	缩写	解释
轮转	ROT	轮转指的是当球在前场的移动/位置致使前导裁判发动一次占位变化或"轮转"至球侧。前导裁判发动轮转的时机是球被移至并停留在了中央裁判一侧（弱侧）。一次前导裁判位置的变化将致使中央裁判（成为"追踪裁判"）和追踪裁判（成为"中央裁判"）的位置变化。
扫视（限制区）	SPA	当前导裁判在端线轮转时，他应当扫视限制区以观察是否发生了无球情况时的非法接触，如果限制区内没有队员，则他应观察将要去的比赛区域。
得分	PG	通过投篮或罚球得分。也指双方球队的最终比分，比如本场比赛比分为 50:47。
记录员	SR	记录员应根据篮球规则的要求填写记录表。
记录表	SS	记录表涵盖了具体及完整的比赛信息。这其中包括球队及队员个人的累积得分和犯规。
掩护	SC	掩护是试图延误或阻止一名不持球的对方队员到达他希望到达的场上位置。
次要（责任区）	SCE	裁判员在确定已覆盖主要责任区的前提下能够覆盖到的责任区和比赛情况。
自我评估	SEF	对自己的表现做出评估的过程。
力判	STC	为了强调一次判罚而大声宣判，强力鸣哨或附加些许手势。这在关键时刻的宣判中比较常见，为的是增加说服力。
无撞人半圆区	NCSC	场上画出无撞人半圆区的目的是为了在篮下的特定位置出现撞人/阻挡情况时能够做出规则解释。无撞人半圆区的界线是无撞人半圆区的一部分。
投篮	N/A	一次朝向球篮的得分尝试。

TERM	ABBR	EXPLANATION
Shot Clock Operator	SCO	The shot clock operator shall be controlling the shot clock according to the basketball rules.
Shot Clock Violation	SCV	Once a team has gained possession of the live ball on the court it is required to attempt a shot within 24/14 seconds. Not to do so is a violation.
Sidelines	N/A	The boundary lines inscribing a side of the playing court area.
Signals	N/A	The official communications as described in the rulebook by which the referees explain their decisions to the players and scorer's table.
Signals (communication among the crew)	N/A	Subtle gesturers made by one referee to the other to help with game maintenance and teamwork – such as enquiring of the other referee if they saw who last touched the ball before it went out of bounds. Each crew may have their own way of communicate internally.
Special Situations	SPS	In the same stopped-clock period that follows an infraction, special situations may arise when additional foul(s) are committed.
Spirit and Intent of the Rules	N/A	The rules were not written to be interpreted literally, but rather, to stop players from gaining an advantage by using illegal methods.Thus, not all contact is a foul - only contact which causes a player to be disadvantaged by the initiator of that contact. Thus, each incident needs to be judged by the effect it has on the game and not in complete isolation. A flexible interpretation of the rules is what is necessary; calling the game by the "spirit and intent" of the rules.
Starting Five	SF	The head coach shall indicate at least 10 minutes before the game the 5 players who are to start the game.
Stay with the Play	SWP	Refers to IOT that referee will not take his/her eyes and concentration off the play before it has ended.
Strong Side (Refereeing/3PO)	SSR	Side of the court where the Lead & Trail referees are located (3PO).

术语	缩写	解释
进攻计时员	SCO	进攻计时员应按照篮球规则的要求操作进攻计时钟。
进攻时间违例	SCV	在场上获得一次新球权（活球）的控球队需要在24/14秒内完成一次投篮。否则则是一起违例。
边线	N/A	指的是球场两边的界线。
手势	N/A	规则手册中所列出的手势是裁判员与队员和记录台解释他们的判罚的交流工具。
手势（裁判员团队之间）	N/A	一名对同伴善于使用信号手势的裁判员能够帮助比赛顺利进行，并加深团队合作——比如当一名裁判员询问同伴们是否看清一起界外球情况中谁最后触球。
特殊情况	SPS	在一次违犯后的停止比赛计时钟期间又发生了一次或多次犯规时，可能出现特殊情况。
规则的精神和意图	N/A	文字规则不能仅仅从书面理解，更应当去观察队员是否通过非法手段而获利。所以并非所有的接触都是犯规，造成身体接触的队员如果致使对方不利，那才是犯规。每一个情况都应通过裁判员判断其对比赛造成的影响而得出结果，不能只看单一片段。规则的弹性解释也是有必要的，要在规则的"精神和意图"下执裁比赛。
首发5人	SF	至少在预定的比赛开始前10分钟，教练员应指明比赛开始上场的5名队员。
看完整个比赛情况	SWP	指的是在个人执裁技巧中，裁判员在一个比赛情况结束之前不应将目光和注意力从中脱离。
强侧（执裁/3人执裁）	SSR	前导裁判和追踪裁判落位的场地一侧（3人执裁）。

TERM	ABBR	EXPLANATION
Substitution Opportunity	SUBO	A substitution opportunity begins when: • For both teams, the ball becomes dead, the game clock is stopped and the referee has ended the communication with the scorer's table. • For both teams, the ball becomes dead following a successful last or only free throw. • For the non-scoring team, a field goal is scored when the game clock shows 2:00 minutes or less in the fourth quarter and in each overtime. A substitution opportunity ends when the ball is at the disposal of a player for a throw-in or a first or only free throw.
Substitution / Substitute	SUB	During playing time, a team member is a substitute when he/she is not on the playing court but is entitled to play.
Switching (Referees)	SW	Refers to switching the positions (roles) of the Lead, Trail and Centre after reporting the foul to the Scorer's Table. The switch normally involves the calling referee moving to a new position on the court.
Table side	TS	This refers to the side of the playing court which is closest to the scorer's table.
Table Officials	TBO	The table officials shall be a scorer, an assistant scorer, a timer and a shot clock operator.
Tap	N/A	A tap is when the ball is directed with the hand(s) towards the opponents' basket.
Team / Team Member	TM	Each team shall consist of: • No more than 12 team members entitled to play, including a captain. • A head coach and, if a team wishes, a first assistant coach. • A maximum of 7 accompanying delegation members who may sit on the team bench and have special responsibilities, e.g. manager, doctor, physiotherapist, statistician, interpreter, etc.
Team Bench Areas	TBA	The team bench areas shall be marked outside the playing court limited by 2 lines. There must be 16 seats available in the team bench area for the team bench personnel which consists of the head coach, the first assistant coach, the substitutes, the excluded players and the team followers. Any other persons shall be at least 2 m behind the team bench.

术语	缩写	解释
替换机会	SUBO	一次替换机会开始： • （对于双方队）当球成死球，比赛计时钟停止，以及裁判员已结束了与记录台的联系时。 • （对于双方队）在最后一次或仅有一次的罚球成功后，球成为死球时。 • （对于非得分队）在第 4 节或每一决胜期的比赛计时钟显示为 2:00 分钟或少于 2:00 分钟，投篮得分时。 一次替换机会结束于掷球入界的队员可处理球时，或第一次或仅有一次的罚球可处理球时。
替补	SUB	在比赛时间内，一名球队成员未在比赛场地上，但他有资格参赛时，是一名替补队员。
换位(裁判)	SW	宣判犯规的前导/追踪/中央裁判在向记录台报告犯规之后须换位。通常来说宣判裁判员都会转换至场上一个新的位置。
记录台侧	TS	指的是最靠近记录台的半边球场。
记录台人员	TBO	记录台人员应是：1 名记录员、1 名助理记录员、1 名计时员和 1 名进攻计时员。
拍	N/A	拍是用手直接把球打向对方球篮。
球队/球队成员	TM	每个队应按下列要求组成： • 不超过 12 名有资格参赛的球队成员，包括一名队长。 • 一名主教练，如果球队需要，可有一名第一助理教练。 • 最多 7 名有专门职责的随队人员可坐在球队席上，如球队管理、医生、理疗师、统计员、翻译等。
球队席区域	TBA	球队席区域应由两条线在场外画出。球队席区域内必须有 16 个座位提供给球队席人员使用。球队席人员包括主教练、第一助理教练、替补队员、出局的队员和随队人员。任何其他人员应在球队席后面至少 2 米处。

TERM	ABBR	EXPLANATION
Team Control (Ball)	TC	Team control starts when a player of that team is in control of a live ball by holding or dribbling it or team has a live ball at their disposal. Team control continues when: 1. A player of that team is in control of a live ball. 2. The ball is being passed between team-mates. Team control ends when: 1. An opponent gains control. 2. The ball becomes dead. 3. The ball has left the player's hand(s) on a shot for a field goal or for a free throw.
Team Control Foul	TCF	An offensive foul. A foul made by a player whose team is in control of the ball at the time.
Team Foul(s)	TFO	A team foul is a personal, technical, unsportsmanlike or disqualifying foul committed by a player. A team is in the team foul penalty situation when it has committed 4 team fouls in a quarter.
Teamwork	N/A	The smooth functioning of the referee team to provide proper coverage and control to a game.
Technical Foul	TF	A foul called on a player, head coach or a substitute or team follower on the bench for unsportsmanlike conduct that involves no contact.(also known as "T").
Tempo	N/A	The speed at which the game is being played: are teams both running up and down the court, fast-breaking and making a lot of mistakes; or, are the teams playing in a deliberate manner in order to make full use of the ball and the shot clock, etc.
Three (3) Person Officiating	3PO	An officiating concept where three referees are working in the game. The terms for the 3 referees are Crew Chief (CC), Umpire 1(U1) and Umpire 2 (U2), and all referees are working during the game in Lead, Trail & Centre positions.
Three (3) seconds	3S	A player shall not remain in the opponents' restricted area for more than 3 consecutive seconds while his/her team is in control of a live ball in the frontcourt and the game clock is running.
Throw-in	T-IN	A throw-in occurs when the ball is passed into the playing court by the out-of- bounds player taking the throw-in.

术语	缩写	解释
球队控制（球）	TC	球队控制球开始于该队一名队员正拿着或运着一个活球，或者可处理一个活球时。 当： 1. 某队一名队员控制一个活球时。 2. 球在同队队员之间传递时。 球队继续控制球。 当： 1. 一名对方队员获得控制球时。 2. 球成死球时。 3. 在投篮或罚球中，球已经离开队员的手时。 球队控制球结束。
控制球队犯规	TCF	一起进攻犯规。即某队员犯规时，该队正控制球。
全队犯规	TFO	全队犯规是指该队队员被判罚的侵人犯规、技术犯规、违反体育运动精神的犯规或取消比赛资格的犯规。在一节中某队全队犯规已发生了4次时，该队处于全队犯规处罚状态。
团队协作	N/A	裁判员团队做出恰当的球场覆盖以及比赛把控的顺畅配合。
技术犯规	TF	技术犯规是指队员、教练员、替补队员或球队席人员因违反体育运动精神的行为所发生的没有身体接触的犯规。
节奏	N/A	比赛进程的速度：指双方球队在场上往返奔跑、快攻以及产生大量失误等，或是双方球队刻意充分运转球打满进攻时间等。
3人裁判	3PO	由三名裁判员执裁比赛的方法。三名裁判员分别是主裁判、第一副裁判和第二副裁判，临场工作时的位置则被称为前导、追踪和中央。
三（3）秒	3S	当某队在前场控制活球并且比赛计时钟正在运行时，该队的队员不得停留在对方队的限制区内超过持续的3秒钟。
掷球入界	T-IN	由界外掷球入界队员将球传入比赛场地内时，掷球入界发生。

111

TERM	ABBR	EXPLANATION
Time & Distance (Basketball)	T&D	When guarding a player who does not control the ball, the elements of time and distance shall apply. A defensive player cannot take a position so near and/or so quickly in the path of a moving opponent that the latter does not have sufficient time or distance either to stop or change his/her direction. The distance is directly proportional to the speed of the opponent, but never less than 1 normal step.
Time-Out (Referees)	RTO	Referees may also call an official time-out when a player has been injured or if they wish to confer with each other, a player, the scorer's table, or team bench.
Time-Out (Team)	TO	A time-out is a one minute break in play where the coach may address their team. Teams may call two time-outs at any time in the first half, three during the second half and 1 per each overtime.
Time-Out Opportunity	TOO	A time-out opportunity begins when: • For both teams, the ball becomes dead, the game clock is stopped and the referee has ended the communication with the scorer's table. • For both teams, the ball becomes dead following a successful last or only free throw. • For the non-scoring team, a field goal is scored. • A time-out opportunity ends when the ball is at the disposal of a player for a throw-in or for a first or only free throw.
Timer	TR	The timer shall measure playing time, time-outs and an interval of play according the Rules of Basketball.
Trail (Referee)	T	Under the dual referee system one referee always leads the play down to the end of the court and the other referee remains close to by slightly behind the play in order to maintain the sandwich principle. It is always the trail referee's responsibility to detect basket interference and to notice whether a shot has gone in or not.
Travelling Violation	TV	When a player with the ball lifts or moves the pivot foot from its spot on the floor before releasing the ball from the hands for a dribble, or takes too many steps after picking up the ball when stopping, passing or shooting. It is not possible to travel while dribbling the ball. During a dribble, there is no limit to the number of steps a player may take when the ball is not in contact with the hands.

术语	缩写	解释
时间与距离	T&D	当防守不控制球的队员时，时间和距离的因素应适用。防守队员不能靠近和/或快速地在移动的对方队员的路径中占据一个位置，以致后者没有足够的时间或距离停步或改变其方向。此距离与对方队员的速度直接成正比，不要少于正常的一步。
暂停（裁判）	RTO	裁判员可以因为如下原因执行一次裁判员暂停：队员受伤，与同伴、队员、记录台或球队席协商。
暂停（球队）	TO	暂停是 1 分钟的比赛中断，期间教练员可与其球队沟通。一支球队可以在上半场的任何时间请求两次暂停，下半场的任何时间请求三次暂停，每一个决胜期可以请求一次暂停。
暂停机会	TOO	当： • （对于双方队）球成死球，比赛计时钟停止以及当裁判员已结束了与记录台的联系时。 • （对于双方队）在最后一次或仅有一次的罚球成功后，球成死球时。 • 对于非得分队，投篮得分时，一次暂停机会开始。 • 当队员在掷球入界或第一次或仅有一次的罚球可处理球时，一次暂停机会结束。
计时员	TR	计时员应根据篮球规则管理比赛时间，暂停时间和比赛休息期。
追踪裁判	T	在两名裁判员临场过程中一名裁判员始终应当在比赛前方首先到达端线，而另一名裁判员则应在比赛后方适当的距离执裁，以此与同伴"包围"所有队员。观察干扰得分和球是否中篮是追踪裁判的责任。
走步违例	TV	一名队员在球离手或开始一次运球前抬起或移动中枢脚，或在结束运球后因急停、传球或投篮时带球行进了超出规则限定的合法步数，一次带球走步违例便发生了。在正常运球时不可能发生带球走步违例。在运球过程中，当球不与队员的手接触时，队员可行进的步数不受限制。

113

TERM	ABBR	EXPLANATION
Triple Whistle	3W	When three referees simultaneously blow their whistles on a same play.
Turnover	TOR	When the offensive team loses possession of the ball other than from a missed or made shot; i.e. an interception, violation or offensive foul.
Two (2) Person Officiating	2PO	A officiating concept where two referees are working in the game. The referees are Crew Chief and Umpire and they are working during the game in Lead and Trail position.
Umpire	U (U1, U2)	Under 2PO, one referee is designated the crew chief and the other the umpire. The umpire is normally the younger and/or less experienced of the two referees. The umpire's duties and prerogatives are the same as the crew chief's with the exceptions noted under the Crew Chief heading in this glossary. Under 3PO, there is a crew chief and two umpires (U1 & U2).
Unsportsmanlike Conduct (Behaviour)	UC	To be unsportsmanlike is to act in a manner unbecoming a fair, ethical, honourable individual. It consists of acts of deceit such; disrespect, such as making debasing or critical remarks about or to a referee or an opponent; vulgarity - such as the use of profanity whether or not directed at someone. The penalty for unsportsmanlike conduct by a player on the court, coach or team member/follower is a technical foul.
Unsportsmanlike Foul	UF	An illegal contact that includes any of the below criteria, should be called as an Unsportsmanlike Foul. • Contact with an opponent and not legitimately attempting to directly play the ball within the spirit and intent of the rules. (C1) • Excessive, hard contact caused by a player in an effort to play the ball or an opponent. (C2) • An unnecessary contact caused by the defensive player in order to stop the progress of the offensive team in transition. This applies until the offensive player begins the act of shooting. (C3)

术语	缩写	解释
三重哨	3W	三名裁判员对同一情况同时鸣哨。
失误	TOR	当进攻队因除了球未中篮／中篮的情况而失去球权的情况是失误。如：被成功抢断球，发生违例或进攻犯规。
2人执裁	2PO	由两名裁判员执裁比赛的方法。两名裁判员分别是主裁判员和副裁判员，临场工作时的位置则被称为前导和追踪。
副裁判	U (U1,U2)	在2人执裁中，两名裁判员分别是主裁判和副裁判。副裁判通常是年轻／相对资历浅的裁判员。副裁判在场上的职责与主裁判相同（除了在规则中另外规定的主裁判权力之外）。在3人执裁中，场上有1名主裁判和两名副裁判（U1和U2）。
违反体育运动精神的行为（行为）	UC	违反体育运动精神行为是指其违背了公平、道德和正大光明的竞赛原则。包含的情况诸如在得知队友应去罚球的情况下故意替罚；表现出不尊重，如对裁判员或对手做出贬低和不公正的评论；粗俗低劣，如口出粗话、脏话（无论朝向某人与否）。对于场上队员／教练员／球队成员／随队人员所做出的违反体育运动精神的行为的判罚应当是一次技术犯规。
违反体育运动精神的犯规	UF	任何达到以下标准的非法接触应被宣判为违反体育精神的犯规。 • 与对方发生身体接触并且不在本规则的精神和意图的范畴内努力比赛。（C1） • 在尽力抢球或在与对方队员尽力争抢中，造成与对方队员过分的严重身体接触。（C2） • 一起攻防转换中，防守队员为了中断进攻队的进攻，与进攻队员造成不必要的身体接触。该原则在进攻队员开始他的投篮动作之前均适用。（C3）

TERM	ABBR	EXPLANATION
Unsportsmanlike Foul	UF	• An illegal contact caused by the player from behind or laterally on an opponent, who is progressing towards the opponent's basket and there are no other players between the progressing player, the ball and the basket. This applies until the offensive player begins the act of shooting. (C4) • Contact by the defensive player on an opponent on the playing court when the game clock shows 2:00 minutes or less in the fourth quarter and in each overtime, when the ball is out-of bounds for a throw-in and still in the hands of the referee or at the disposal of the player taking the throw-in. (C5)
Video Operator	VO	The video operators tag the calls of the referees in FIBA competitions. Their main function is to capture data through the referees' calls, with the support of a computer and other devices, for a subsequent analysis of the images and statistical data of the actions called by the referees.
Violation	N/A	A violation is an infraction of the rules. Penalty: The ball shall be awarded to the opponents for a throwin at the place nearest to the infraction, except directly behind the backboard, unless otherwise stated in the rules.
Warning	WAR	It refers to any situation when the referees determinate that a head coach or player should be warned for an incorrect conduct: normally for inproper behaviour, delay of game, fake.
Weak Side (Refereeing)	WSR	Side of the court where the Centre referee is located (in 3PO).
Wiping the Basket	N/A	Cancelling the score (normally used in North America)
Working Area	WA	Area in which a referee in any given position normally operates.

术语	缩写	解释
违反体育运动精神的犯规	UF	• 一起对方队员从正朝着对方球篮行进的队员身后或侧面与其造成的非法接触，并且在该行进队员、球和对方球篮之间没有其他队员。该原则在进攻队员开始他的投篮动作之前均适用。（C4） • 在第 4 节和每一决胜期比赛计时钟显示 2:00 分钟或更少，当掷球入界的球在界外并且仍在裁判员手中，或掷球入界队员可处理时，防守队员在比赛场内对进攻队员造成身体接触。（C5）
即时回放专员	VO	即时回放专员在所有国际篮联比赛中负责记录裁判员的每一次宣判。他们的主要工作是利用电脑或其他电子设备来通过裁判员的宣判抓取数据，为的是收集裁判员宣判的图像和数据以供后续分析。
违例	N/A	违例是违犯规则。罚则：将球判给对方队员在最靠近发生违例的地点掷球入界，但在篮板正后方除外，除非规则另有规定。
警告	WAR	指的是裁判员给予主教练或队员唯一的一次因其不正当行为而得到的警告：通常是不合理的行为、延误比赛或假摔。
弱侧(执裁)	WSR	中央裁判落位的一侧（3 人执裁）。
挥手示意无效	N/A	取消得分（通常在北美地区使用）。
工作区域	WA	裁判员在场上常规执裁时应当所处的位置区域。

NOTE

NOTE